D0116875

First English edition published by Colour Library Books Ltd.
© 1983 Text: Colour Library Books Ltd., Guildford, Surrey, England.
© 1983 Illustrations: Keystone Press Agency, London, England.
This edition is published by Crescent Books
Distributed by Crown Publishers, Inc.
hgfedcba
Printed by Jisa-Rieusset, bound by Eurobinder-Barcelona-Spain
ISBN 0 517 424517
All rights reserved
CRESCENT 1983

JOHN FITZGERALD
KENNEDY

A PHOTOGRAPHIC TRIBUTE

Bill Harris

CRESCENT

"For heaven's sake, they have crummy things it goes on for an hour. They have good things it goes on for five minutes."

A six year-old spectator, Kennedy airport speech, Fort Dodge, Iowa, September 22, 1960

The speech was only about five minutes long. After acknowledging a long friendship with Congressman Merwin Coad and boosting the Senatorial campaign of Governor Herschel

Loveless and reminding his audience that he was following in the footsteps of former President Harry S. Truman, Senator Kennedy launched into an attack on the Republican record on farm income. The speech was stopped for mild applause five times, only twice for laughter and the bigger of the two laughs was for a quote from Harry Truman who had said that farmers who voted Republican in 1952 may have gotten what they deserved.

The other laugh was at the expense of his opponent, Richard M. Nixon, who the Senator quoted as having said that the unpopular Secretary of Agriculture, Ezra Taft Benson, was the greatest secretary in history. Without a pause, Kennedy added: "and Mr. Nixon is a truthful man."

From then on it was a perfectly ordinary campaign speech, directed at the pocketbooks of Iowa farmers. Not much to inspire a six year-old girl to cry for more.

What she said that day could easily be John F. Kennedy's

When Joseph Kennedy was Ambassador to Britain, the comings and goings of his nine children were reported as regularly as his own. The 1944 wedding of daughter Kathleen to Marquis Huntington, son of the Duke of Devonshire, though not popular with the family, was a hit with the British people.

epitaph. What he said that day could, if they had nothing more to go on than printed words, leave future historians scratching their heads. More often than not, Kennedy the candidate and Kennedy the President inspired his audiences not so much by what he said as by the way he said it. Before 1960, the word charisma wasn't used much outside theological circles where it described a divinely inspired talent or a special quality of leadership. It wasn't invented for John F. Kennedy, but somehow no other word would do.

Kennedy the campaigner was as

close as many of us will get to understanding the zeal of the Biblical evangelists. His speeches were short and to the point, a real novelty to audiences who had been accustomed to long-winded politicians. He was relaxed, confident, earnest. Though he is often remembered for his wit, his speeches never had them rolling in the aisles. He made it a point to use plenty of quotes from statesmen and famous writers running the gamut from T. S. Eliot to Benjamin Disraeli. And he was among the first to mention his opponent by name, breaking an unwritten rule that was a

As young boys and as young men, Jack Kennedy and his brothers knew important people in world affairs as well as in the world of business thanks to their father's broad influence in both areas. Not exactly an Abe Lincoln boyhood, but important to the young man who would later become the leader of the free world.

cornerstone of American politics.

None of it was accidental. Though he was running against Richard Nixon, Nixon was running on the record of President Dwight D. Eisenhower, one of the great father figures of American history. Though Kennedy broke tradition by attacking Nixon directly, he made it a point never to mention the man whose job he was working so hard to capture. In a television debate with Nixon, the name Eisenhower came up and Kennedy couldn't avoid a response. But he quickly softened it by adding that he was much more concerned with the future than with the past.

It was the kind of thing his audiences loved to hear. They were, in the main, young people. Like Kennedy himself they had come of age during and after World War II. Indeed, many of his enthusiastic supporters had no memory of the war at all. And his critics gloated over the fact that time after time the bulk of his audiences were teenage girls who weren't able to vote and young mothers who probably wouldn't take the time. They were there, the experts said, to see the

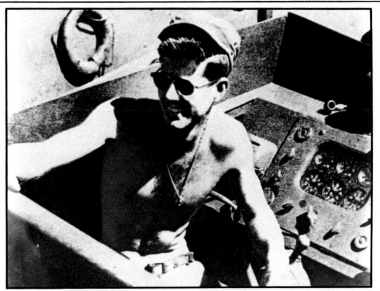

they waited anyway, and then, like the crowds at all the stops before them, held him there making him even later for the next one.

"Yes, he's attracting big crowds," said the Republicans, "but it's just a bunch of kids." And it did seem true. Even the Democrats had to admit that. But if he wasn't attracting anybody over forty-five, there were bona fide voters in those crowds even though the Grand Old Party wrote them off as "kids."

They elected him, of course. Not exactly a landslide, but good enough to change the style of a country and to help set the stage for an era that will always be remembered as a time when the young people of the world stood

The Kennedy family accompanied the Ambassador to most formal occasions and stood solidly behind him in his public life. Though dedicated to avoiding World War II, he gave his sons to the cause after the U.S. became involved. Jack went into the Navy and served in the Pacific.

handsome young candidate and not to hear what he had to say. So much for charisma.

But his audiences, like the six year-old in Fort Dodge, usually found themselves wishing for more when the candidate moved on for his next speech.

During the 1960 campaign, Kennedy averaged between ten and fifteen speeches a day, very few of them more than ten minutes long. But in spite of that, any talk scheduled past noon was usually to an audience that had been waiting in the hot sun or the rain for more than an hour beyond the appointed time. By dinner time that delay was almost always doubled. But

up to be counted.

Less than two weeks before his inauguration, in a speech before the Massachusetts Legislature, the President-Elect called on Pericles for the words to describe the new Administration: "We do not imitate – for we are a model to others."

In the same speech, he also told the legislators: "It was here in Massachusetts my grandparents were born – it is here I hope my grandchildren will be born."

The new President's grandparents were well-known to everyone in that room. Both his grandfathers had been forces to be reckoned with in the politics of "the Boston Irish," a society as distinguishable from other Irish-

In 1938, young Bobby Kennedy was the toast of London. In 1944, his older brother Joe died in action in an attempt to help stop one of the worst phases of the London bombing by V-rockets.

Americans as from the non-Irish population of Boston.

Both of Kennedy's grandfathers had served in this same State Legislature. P. J. Kennedy, his father's father, served in both houses; his mother's father, John F. Fitzgerald, went from the Legislature to the United States Congress, ran twice for the U.S. Senate and was the first son of Irish immigrants to become Mayor of Boston – a feat that made him quite famous back in the Old Country, and the pride of County Wexford where his parents had been born, because all over Ireland, Boston was well-known as "The Hub of the Universe."

Fitzgerald had a bunch of nicknames. Some people called him "Honey," others "Fitz." He

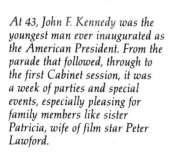

At 43, John F. Kennedy was the youngest man ever inaugurated as the American President. From the parade that followed, through to the first Cabinet session, it was a week of parties and special events, especially pleasing for family members like sister Patricia, wife of film star Peter Lawford.

was often called "The Little General," sometimes just plain "John F." In 1915, after he was given an honorary doctorate by Notre Dame University, a lot of his admirers began calling him "Doctor". He was born in Boston's North End, the ward that eventually made him its boss. At that time, in 1863, the Irish population in Boston was well over 50,000 and growing.

That same year, 1964, Robert was elected to the Senate from New York.

The swearing-in of the new Cabinet, including brother Robert as Attorney General, was the first of many important occasions for the new President and the First Lady. Brother Edward Kennedy, would fill his brother's seat in the Senate and then retake it in a landslide more impressive than Jack's history-making margin in 1958.

dingy tenement that had no bathroom or electric lights or any other convenience – not even a humble accordion, let alone a piano or a harmonium – and when my dear mother and father went to their reward, I had to take care of all of my brothers. I washed dishes, made beds, sifted ashes and

In March, 1961, the President went to Vienna to meet with Soviet Premier Khruschev and often met in Washington with Foreign Minister Andrei Gromyko. His wife, Jacqueline, was almost always at his side.

As often happens in political life, a man's life story gets salted with incidents that may or may not be the whole truth. It is true that young Johnny was one of a family of nine sons, each about two years apart in age. "We were like steps in a stairs," he once recalled. Most of his audiences believed he was the eldest, probably because of this capsule biography he regularly delivered at political gatherings:

"I was born on the top floor of a

brought up scuttles of coal and firewood, climbing three flights of creaky stairs. For some reason or other it was my trust to boss the family. I even washed the faces of the older boys every day and oftentimes dressed them. I remember that I used to accompany my mother when she bought her millinery from Kate Haley, or to the Jordan Marsh Company where she bought socks and under-clothing for the family, and in that way I got experience which served me well. After feeding them and sending them off to school I would go out and earn money to keep the family

together."

When he finished telling them that, there probably wasn't a dry eye in the place. Most of the people he was talking to had similar experiences. He, at least, had the advantage of a formal education. He had gone to Boston Latin School, the same school, he

was pleased to tell his audiences, that had educated Benjamin Franklin. He had made a name for himself there as a right fielder on the baseball team, as captain of the football team and as editor of the school's magazine. In his spare time, he was active in neighborhood athletic groups, one

Meetings with the Soviet Premier in the company of Secretary of State Dean Rusk or Foreign Minister Gromyko, though not completely cordial, often evoked public smiles on the part of the principals as well as the First Lady.

13

of which made him captain of its polo team, of all things.

He was a student at Harvard Medical School when his father died. It wasn't uncommon in Boston in those days for large families of children to suddenly find themselves orphaned, but the tradition was for aunts or sisters to take on the responsibility of raising them. Unfortunately, Tom Fitzgerald had fathered only sons. "I could not allow our little home to be broken up," recalled Honey Fitz in an interview many years later, so he dropped out of college and became father and mother to his brothers.

That was 1881, not a terrific time for an 18 year-old Irish boy to throw himself on Boston's labor market. But young Johnny knew where his opportunities lay. He couldn't get a job in a bank,

Visiting her sister, Princess Lee Radziwill, in London, or babies in a Paris hospital; presenting a trophy to the Argentine Equestrian Team or visiting with Greek Premier Karamanlis, Mrs. Kennedy's impression on the world was almost as great as the one her husband created in speaking appearances before Congress.

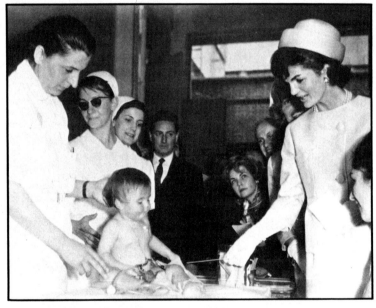

obviously. In fact, almost any white collar job was out of the question. And so the boy who had dreamed of becoming a doctor decided to get into an entirely different field: politics.

He was a natural. He was a bouncy, smiling man who, like his grandson, could spellbind a political audience. He didn't smoke, he didn't drink, he loved people and people loved him. And when all else failed, he'd captivate them with an Irish tenor rendition of "Sweet Adeline". If Jack Kennedy had a talent for public relations and promotions, he owed a great deal of it to this grandfather. When Fitz was elected Mayor, he began one of the country's first advertising campaigns to build his city up as a

tourist attraction. He staged trade shows to lure business there and gave financial support to tour bus operators.

One of the beneficiaries of that program was a young Harvard graduate who operated sightseeing buses from South Station. His name was Joseph P. Kennedy. Joe's father was P. J. Kennedy,

ward boss in East Boston. But young Kennedy had more to thank the Mayor for than the city's support of his new business. Joe had fallen in love with Fitz's daughter, Rose. Fitz liked that idea a lot. He himself had the power to deliver votes in the North End, Kennedy could do the same in East Boston. That, coupled with

the fact that he was an incredibly popular Mayor, meant he was virtually assured a second term.

But nothing is certain in politics. Out of the blue, Congressman James Michael Curley, himself a product of the ward boss tradition, announced that he was going to clear the rascals out; that he was running for Mayor of Boston. The men who controlled the vote

As godfather for his wife's neice, greeting Premier Ikeda of Japan in the company of former president Eisenhower, welcoming Konrad Adenauer of the Federal Republic of West Germany, presenting an award to West Berlin Mayor Willy Brandt, the young President led a very busy ceremonial life. Fortunately, his 28-year-old brother Edward was able to handle some of those details for him, including a 1961 trip to Italy and an audience with Pope John XXIII and receiving the Milanese version of the Keys to the City from Lord Mayor Cassinis.

panicked and Curley was elected. Needless to say, the old system died that day in 1913 when the votes were counted.

Curley had called himself a "reform" candidate. It's a word that crops up often in city politics. More often than not, the reform is not much more than a shifting of power from one faction to another. In the beginning Curley had been a ward boss himself, which is why the others panicked when he stood for Mayor. He knew where the bodies were buried.

When he became Mayor, he and Fitzgerald became arch-enemies. Where there had been four ward bosses to control the city, including John F. Kennedy's two grandfathers, there was now one,

and, of course, James Michael Curley went on to become a textbook definition of a political boss. Voters looking for favors in the past had gone to their local leader. With Curley in charge, they went directly to City Hall.

Even without Curley, the old system probably would have died anyway. The Irish in Boston were into their second generation and the grandsons of immigrants resented being told how to cast their votes. It had been quite different with their parents.

To say that life in Boston for a

While his brother, the President, was making historic speeches and press conference announcements, Ted Kennedy's Italian tour took him to the international exposition, Italia '61, where various officials showed him aspects of the history and the future of their country.

mid-nineteenth century immigrant from Ireland was harsh would be the understatement of this century. Their living conditions, according to an official city study, were so bad that "there can be no cleanliness, privacy or proper ventilation. With the ignorance, carelessness and generally loose and dirty habits which prevail among the occupants, the necessary evils are greatly increased in both amount and intensity. In Broad Street and all the surrounding neighborhood, the situation of the Irish is particularly wretched. This whole district is a perfect hive of human beings, without comforts and without common necessities. In many cases they are huddled together like brutes without regard to sex or age or sense of decency. Grown men and women sleep together in the same apartment, and sometimes wife and husband, brothers and sisters in the same bed. Under such circumstances, self-respect, forethought, all high and noble virtues soon die out and sullen indigence and despair, or disorder, intemperance and utter degradation reign supreme."

But if there was no room for them in this city that had already matured, there was also open hostility among the established families. Boston had been founded by Protestant Englishmen looking for religious freedom. As often

happens, once they found their freedom, they set out to deny it to others. Catholics especially were not wanted. There was no abundance of available jobs, either, and without help, an immigrant without a needed trade simply couldn't find employment.

Help came in the form of the ward bosses.

In 1847, in a debate in the State Legislature, a Boston politician told his fellow statesmen that the Irish were displacing too many "honest" workers. "They are taking jobs away from the respectable laborers of the State," he shouted, "and from their manner of living they work for much less per day, being satisfied with food to support animal existence alone while the latter not

Quiet family moments under the White House Christmas tree are rare for a President. But President Kennedy also seemed to find joy in a warm handshake with Prince Bernhard of the Netherlands or an anecdote by Greek Premier Karamanlis. The First Lady later visited Greece and its Queen, Frederika.

While the President showed off the White House to such personages as Britain's Prime Minister Harold Macmillan or presented awards to people like nuclear physicist Hans Bethe, Jacqueline Kennedy often went off to New York on shopping expeditions. But sometimes she took on the role of official greeter herself as was the case when Pakistani President Mohammed Ayub Khan came to Washington and both appeared in ceremonial gold garlands.

only labor for the body but for the mind, the soul and the State." Such things contrived to keep the Irish apart and out of the mainstream, but it also forced them to stand together. A man can't become a hero unless there is a good villain to fight. The Irish in Boston had plenty of both. And the best of the former managed to become City Aldermen. Their first and most important role was to tell newcomers that they had a duty to their families to become naturalized citizens and to participate in the political process.

Between 1850 and 1855 the number of naturalized Irish voters nearly quadrupled in Boston while the rest of the population accounted for an increase in the voting rolls of less that 15 per cent. And the organizers among the Irish, who had convinced them to register to vote, worked hard to make sure they all showed up at the polls on election day. They weren't above telling their new constituents how to vote, of course, but that wasn't really necessary. There were no social organizations to help the poor and the sick and the unemployed back then, and the ward bosses took on the role themselves. If the aldermen could help it, nobody had to go without firewood or a crust of bread or some sort of job.

While they were an influence for good in their own wards, their counterparts in other parts of the city weren't all that happy and in the 1850s they began a campaign of hate against the Irish that is one of the saddest chapters in American history.

When the Republican-supported candidate for Governor was

defeated in 1856, word spread like wildfire that they had no one to blame but the Irish-Catholics. Over the previous several years, the Republicans had tried several ways to clip the Irish wings. They had toyed with such ideas as making it illegal for paupers to vote, making it necessary to live in Massachusetts for 21 years before being able to become a citizen, and they pushed hard for the old stand-by of making literacy a requirement of voting. Their

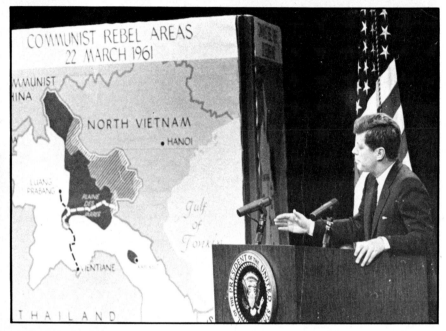

Clockwise from top left: Meeting with the Ambassador from Mauritania; with General Douglas MacArthur; Edward Kennedy with the wife of the Lord Mayor of Milan; a press conference to explain the situation in Southeast Asia; with South Korea's General Park; the 1961 State of The Union Message.

defeat at the polls finally unified them and over the next two years they were able to get laws on the books that made the ability to read the State Constitution (just read, mind you, not to understand; only lawyers were required to do that) and to write pre-requisites to being able to vote. Later on, when they realized that large numbers of Irish immigrants could read and write, they added another law: that a naturalized citizen had to wait two years before being able to vote.

They were very satisfied with themselves after that. Two years isn't 21 years, but it was a significant step in the right direction. What they didn't realize was that such laws only served to solidify the power of the ward bosses in Boston's Irish neighborhoods. In 1851, many of the Irish had become disenchanted with some of the ideas of the State Democrats and responded by breaking ranks with the Party. The antics of the State Republicans five

Clockwise from top left: The First Lady on a tour of the Greek Islands; an award ceremony in honor of the pilots who tested the X-15 aircraft; a ceremony establishing the Dag Hammerskjold Chair of Government and Law at Leopoldville; a visit to Supreme Headquarters Allied Powers Europe in 1961.

years later convinced them that their best interests were better served by Democrats, though, and by the time John Fitzgerald and P. J. Kennedy rose to power there was no question that they or their descendants would ever switch to the Republican Party.

By the 1890s when Kennedy and Fitzgerald arrived on the political scene, the Irish clearly dominated it. But they still weren't accepted among the "natives." Nor were their constituents. And the harder the Establishment tried to put them down, the more powerful the Irish leaders became.

When Curley took over as Mayor, the game changed. The bosses he overturned had built a power base by helping people who needed help, confident that simple

Kennedy was the youngest elected President. His predecessor, Dwight D. Eisenhower, who left office at age 70, was the oldest. Kennedy's family was young, too. Daughter Caroline was two when she moved into the White House; John F. Kennedy, Jr. was born in 1960. Their mother, Jacqueline, helped the whole country feel young during her White House years. The youthful appearance of the brothers Edward, Robert and John often stood in sharp contrast with such world leaders as West German Chancellor Konrad Adenauer.

gratitude could be translated into votes. Curley did the same thing, of course, but extended his power by turning hate against the opposition.

When he was a Senator, John F. Kennedy recalled that in the last century, "each wave of immigrants disliked and distrusted the next. The English said the Irish 'kept the Sabbath and everything else they could lay their hands on.' The English and the Irish distrusted the Germans who 'worked too hard,' The English and the Irish and the Germans disliked the Italians; and the Italians joined their predecessors in disparaging the

Slavs."

Curley turned all that to advantage. During campaigns, he regularly called upon the deep-seated Irish-Catholic distrust of Protestants. One Irishman he didn't like lost an election after Curley circulated a rumor that he had been seen eating a roast beef sandwich on a Friday. In another case, he told a newspaper that a Catholic candidate was

contemplating leaving his wife and children to take up with a 16 year-old girl. Neither was able to rise above the charges. Nor was the poor man Curley hit with the most disastrous charge of all: that he had secretly become a 32-degree Freemason.

He regularly hired strong-arm men to disrupt or control political rallies. At one of them, when a heckler stood up to challenge him,

Curley calmly said, "Sir, there are ladies present and you are speaking without removing your derby. If you would take if off, we all will listen to you." Without thinking, the man took off the plug hat, and without a bit of hesitation. a Curley goon hit him on the head with a blackjack.

His men didn't need a rally to perform their dirty tricks. During one campaign, he sent them out in waves through Irish neighborhoods in the middle of the night. Their assignment was to knock on doors, identify themselves as Baptist clergymen and make a pitch for the opposition candidate.

Curley's battles with Honey Fitz came to a head on the first day of his term in City Hall. Among Fitzgerald's accomplishments as Mayor had been the addition of a new wing to City Hall. He also took pride in the fact that he had upgraded the city's fire hydrant

The President's face was familiar all over the world, and so was that of his wife. On the preceding page, she's seen (clockwise from top left) with: Mrs. Indira Gandhi in India; with a baby elephant named "Drvashi"; with an official welcoming party in London; with Indian Prime Minister Nehru; with members of the Diplomatic Corps (and her husband) in Washington; being hugged (twice!) by her brother-in-law, Prince Stanislaus Radziwill; and with Pope John XXIII at the Vatican.

system. Curley called attention to both by opening the hydrants and flooding the new wing. "Just cleaning house," announced the Reform Mayor.

The battle between the two men would continue for the rest of their lives. Before he died, Curley was elected Mayor of Boston in four separate elections. He was defeated three times. In the meantime, he served a term as Governor and went back to serve another term in Congress. During that time he also spent five months in the Federal Penitentiary at Danbury, Connecticut, having been convicted on conspiracy charges in a case against a confidence man who had been found guilty of mail fraud.

By the time Curley went to jail, Fitzgerald was in his eighties and enjoying the status of elder statesman. The feud continued, though. Curley was eventually set free by an order issued by President Harry S. Truman. The order had been inspired by a petition submitted by Massachusetts Democrats in

Congress. All of them had signed it, except one; John F. Kennedy.

Congressman Jack Kennedy was responding to an inviolate family rule that what happens to one member of the clan happens to all. Mr. Curley was twice blessed.

P. J. Kennedy was another of the "rascals" Curley told the voters he was dedicated to eliminating. In the case of Jack Kennedy's

In 1962, Robert Kennedy went to Germany where he toured the City of Berlin with Mayor Willy Brandt and received a Freedom Bell Award from him. He also visited the Cathedral at Cologne, and placed a wreath at the Berlin monument to the memory of Ida Siekmann, who died rather than accept a forced return to East Germany.

paternal grandfather, Curley was successful.

Pat Kennedy was only five years older than Fitz, but many said he was a generation behind him in the changing world of politics. He was born in East Boston, the son of an immigrant father who died four years later. Like so many of his neighbors, he went to work early in life and was able to save enough money to buy a saloon, but not enough to hire a bartender. That was no problem, he was good at that himself. In fact, if you were asked to describe what you thought a Boston bartender looked like in the 1870s, chances are good you'd describe young Pat Kennedy. He was five feet ten inches tall, weighed 185 pounds and sported a handlebar

The Attorney General and his wife, Ethel, went from West Germany to Paris where he was greeted with a friendly handshake from his French counterpart, Minister of Justice, Bernard Chenot. A few months later Robert Kennedy went to Japan for a meeting with Prime Minister Ikeda.

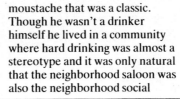

moustache that was a classic. Though he wasn't a drinker himself he lived in a community where hard drinking was almost a stereotype and it was only natural that the neighborhood saloon was also the neighborhood social

center.

Not only was business good, but the man behind the bar was as important to the men who came there as their parish priest. Probably more so; not many of them went to confession under the

influence of alcohol. There weren't many men in the East Boston ward Kennedy didn't know, and very few who hadn't come to regard him as a man to turn to when they needed help. He didn't disappoint them. And in the process he became boss of the ward after winning a seat on the Democratic Committee.

New arrivals from Ireland brought him new problems, but they brought new opportunities, too. In 1885 he was elected to the Massachusetts House of Representatives, a post he held for five consecutive terms, followed by two terms as a State Senator.

He never ran for office again after that, but quietly continued to gather power in Boston. In fact, until Curley came along, he was one of the small group that controlled the city. Together they hand-picked mayors and commissioners, decided who would go to the State House and to

The result was that, over the years, P. J. Kennedy was identified as an important man to see if you needed a job or favor taken care of. In the process he also developed good connections in what they call "the private sector"

At the end of 1962, while the President was presenting an award to General Lyman Lemnitzer, Chairman of the Joint Chiefs of Staff, and his brother Edward was visiting President Allstein of the European Economic Community, Jacqueline Kennedy and daughter Caroline enjoyed an Italian holiday at Ravello.

today. At the same time, he wasn't above accepting city jobs for himself. At various times he was Fire Commissioner, a Commissioner of Elections and a Wire Commissioner. His ethics were never ever questioned, but a contemporary once said that "Pretty much every day of his life he has done something for the political betterment of Patrick J. Kennedy."

P. J. had a flair for politics, but his real forte was as a businessman. Before he became a State Representative, he sold his tavern

Italian photographers, famous for such things, didn't give the First Lady a moment's rest. Her sister, Princess Lee Radziwill, and son Anthony accompanied Jacqueline and Caroline on their visit to the Amalfi Coast.

and went into the wholesale liquor business. He also owned a coal company which helped him in his political activities, because keeping warm in a New England winter was as important to most of his constituents as finding a job. While he was serving in the Legislature he also helped organize two banks, clients for which he found in the East Boston ward that gave him his political power.

Many of the Kennedy biographers say that P.J. was

town, serving in the Legislature and running a successful business. The boy didn't have a financial worry in the world, but he loved to make money. It all started with a desire to be "one of the boys," taking odd jobs that would make him more like the other kids in school who needed to peddle papers and run errands to help keep food on the family table. From the day he earned the first dime of his own he was obsessed with a desire to make more. He worked on a sightseeing boat before he was a teenager and as soon as he was old enough went to work for his father's bank as a messenger. Like his future father-in-law, Honey Fitzgerald, he went to Boston Latin School, and like

Going to church, water-skiing or just strolling, their every move was accompanied by clicking shutters.

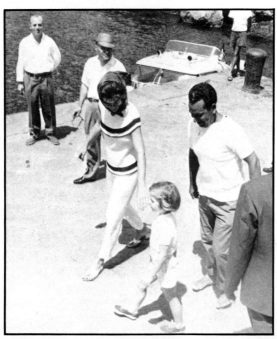

better at business than politics, probably because his style of politics went out of vogue before they were born. The truth is he was a master of both. The business empire he began still thrives, thanks to his son Joseph P. Kennedy. As a politician, he is unique for having been remembered, even by his political enemies, as an honest and decent man.

By the time his son Joe was born, P.J. was a very powerful man, living in the best part of

Fitz became captain of the school's baseball team. In fact, his future father-in-law gave him a special award during his senior year, in recognition of his record as the best hitter of any high school baseball player in town.

Joe Kennedy followed Fitz's footsteps from Boston Latin into Harvard, too. But, unlike the Mayor, he went on to graduate, a rare thing for a boy with an Irish background in 1912. During his years as a student, he kept his hand in the business world. It was during this period that he bought his first sightseeing bus. A year later he bought another and during the following summer vacation ran the business from out of town. He had taken another job playing semi-professional baseball in the White Mountains and, as though he had

Before her return to the United States for an appointment with a nuclear submarine, the <u>Marquis De Lafayette</u>, Mrs. Kennedy stopped in Rome to meet Italian President Gronchi. The President, meanwhile, met with Crown Prince Massan of Libya. He also tossed out the first ball to open the new stadium in Washington, an event he enjoyed so much he went back a few weeks later and did it again.

to supplement his income, he had also taken a side job as an out-of-town reporter for a Boston newspaper.

As if all that wasn't enough to keep his mind occupied, he was also courting Mayor Fitzgerald's daughter, Rose. They had known each other practically all their lives, but there was plenty of competition for her hand, including another Harvard man who flew his own airplane.

But Joe Kennedy was doing

some serious flying of his own.

His interest in money naturally led him to an interest in banking. He worked in his father's bank for a while after graduation until his father engineered a better job for him as assistant bank examiner for the State. In the process he got to know who was who and what was what in the banking business in Massachusetts. Two years later he found out that the Columbia Trust, one of the banks his father had helped establish, was considering

And now that the young man she preferred was president of his own bank, it was hard for Fitzgerald to come up with a reasonable objection. Joe and Rose were married less than a year later.

Ironically, Joe had to borrow the down payment for their first house, but he didn't mind. The house was in Brookline, a suburb that was previously the private turf of Protestants. It was the kind of thumb-in-the-eye Joe Kennedy loved.

He gave the Mayor a thumb-in-the-eye less than ten months later when he named their first child

selling out to another neighborhood bank. It was an opportunity too good to miss. In a short time, he borrowed enough money from a lot of friends to buy the bank himself. Once having done that, he made himself its president. He was 24 years old and on his way to becoming a millionaire on his own.

Rose Fitzgerald's father and Joe Kennedy's father were never what you'd call close friends, though each was forced to spend a lot of time with the other. Fitz had other people in mind for a son-in-law, but his daughter never really did.

Clockwise from top left: With British Prime Minister Harold Macmillan; with British Foreign Secretary Lord Home; inspecting a guard of honor in Bermuda; with Crown Prince Faisal of Saudi Arabia; with German Ambassador Dr. Wilhelm Grewe; with President Olympio of Togo.

Joseph P. Kennedy, Jr. rather than John Francis after his grandfather. The slight was corrected two years later, on May 29, 1917, when they named their second son John Fitzgerald Kennedy.

On the same day, Joe Kennedy's business career got another boost upward with his appointment to the board of the Massachusetts

Electric Company. It was his golden opportunity, he explained, to "meet people like the Saltonstalls" and other members of the old Boston Establishment, most of whom were still hostile to Irish Catholics no matter how good their heads for business or politics.

Not long after the start of the First World War, opportunity

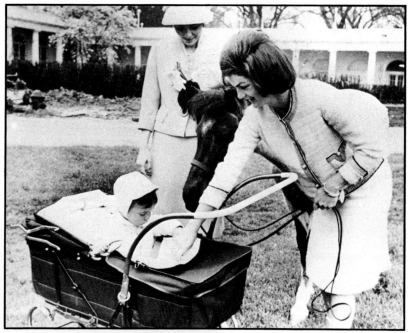

Clockwise from top left: The TV announcement of the Cuban blockade; Jacqueline riding with Pakistan's President Ayub Khan; the First Lady on a New York visit; with the Empress of Persia and Caroline's pony, Macaroni; with son John and the Empress; the President with Pote Sarasin, of the Southeast Asia Treaty Organization; and with Sir Garfield Barwick, Australian Minister for External Affairs.

Clockwise from top left: With President Mohammed Zaher of Afghanistan; with James J. O'Keefe, Lord Mayor of Dublin; with Indian President Sarvepalli Radhakrishnan; announcing the Cuban blockade.

knocked again in the form of a $20,000 a year job as assistant manager of Bethlehem Steel's giant shipyard at Quincy. When the war was over the job got dull and so he joined the investment firm of Hayden Stone at half the salary. On the side, he went into a partnership with some friends to buy control of 31 movie theaters in New England, which led to the acquisition of the franchise for Universal Pictures in the area.

His Hayden Stone connection taught him how to manipulate the stock market for his own advantage, a valuable bit of knowledge for a young man who wanted nothing as much as to be a millionaire.

He became one. But he was still too "Irish" for the people everyone thought really mattered in Boston. "Boston is no place to bring up children," he sniffed – he had five to bring up by then – "besides, if you want to make money, you should go where the money is." With that, he bought a house in

then, he set out to get richer.

This was the Roaring Twenties, when all sorts of people in New York were getting rich in all sorts of ways. Kennedy decided the best way for him to do it was to get into show business. He had already gotten a taste of the movie industry with his chain of theaters in Northern New England. When he heard that a British firm was anxious to sell an American subsidiary that produced Hollywood movies, he sold some of his theaters and rounded up financial help from a group of friends, including former Mayor

Clockwise from top left: With King Vatthana of Laos; with Italian Parliament leader Giuseppe Saragat; Robert Kennedy in 1963; Edward Kennedy announcing he would run for Congress in the 1964 election.

New York and ceremoniously moved his family there in a private railroad car.

The house he bought was in a section of the Bronx called Riverdale. It didn't matter a bit to the people there if you were Irish. Even Boston Irish. It mattered a lot if you were rich. And though Joe Kennedy was very rich by

Fitzgerald, who just loved the idea of rubbing elbows with the likes of Louis B. Mayer and Sam Goldwyn.

But Kennedy didn't cast himself in the mold of a movie mogul. He was in this business, just as was the case with every other business he involved himself in, to make money, nothing more.

The people who ran Hollywood in the mid-'20s weren't opposed to turning a profit, of course, but most considered movie making an art form. Kennedy let them go on thinking that and began churning out westerns and steamy romances at the rate of one a week and at a cost per picture of about one-tenth the amount his competitors were

spending. The "art" that interested him most was the engraving of George Washington on dollar bills.

He had no illusions, though. When a newsman once remarked that his company had turned out some good pictures, Kennedy was incredulous. "Name one," he challenged.

His hard-nosed approach to

cutting costs and to making the film industry more businesslike made him wealthy beyond his own wildest dreams and dramatically changed the young industry. By the time the next dramatic change, talking pictures, hit Hollywood, Joe Kennedy was way ahead of the trend. A friend had introduced him to a young man named David Sarnoff who was establishing a new company called Radio Corporation of America. When producers began tinkering with talkies they passed RCA by and Sarnoff didn't like that a bit. He broke into the Hollywood market by buying a block of stock in Kennedy's company. Kennedy, meanwhile, had gotten control of the Keith-Albee-Orpheum theater chain, and by 1928, after a series of complicated transactions, put the whole thing under a new umbrella called Radio-Keith-Orpheum.

The new company, RKO, became an RCA subsidiary and Joe Kennedy "retired." But he did more than count his money. He became a film producer of the type he had once scorned. He joined forces with Gloria Swanson to produce a film called *Sadie Thompson* based on Somerset Maugham's *Rain*. They did several other movies together, each breaking the Kennedy rule of producing as cheaply as possible to assure the highest possible profit. By 1930 he "retired" again, after losing what was described loosely as "millions." Miss Swanson said years later that Kennedy didn't lose a dime, but that all the money that went down the drain was hers.

True or not, he knew enough to move on to better things.

By this point in his life, the public relations men had taken over and sorting out the truth isn't easy. But most agree that he increased his personal fortune by more than $5 million in his Hollywood ventures. Meanwhile, by the late '20s he was getting to be more and more active in the stock market. Who wasn't in those days? But he was smarter than the average investor, and by the time the market crashed in 1929 he was well out of it. In fact, some of his critics said that his eagerness to sell contributed to the crash. Why did he get out when everyone else was so eager to get in? His own

explanation, undoubtedly inspired by a clever PR man, was: "I dropped into a shoeshine parlor on Wall Street one day. The shoeshine boy didn't know who I was. He wasn't looking for information or fishing for a tip. He was just an average wage-earner playing the market like everyone else. He looked up at me as he snapped the cloth over my shoes and told me what was going to happen to various stocks and offerings that day. I listened as I looked down at him, and when I left the place I thought, 'When the time comes that a shoeshine boy knows as much as I do about what is going on in the stock market, tells me so and is entirely correct,

Opposite page: A White House ceremony before 200 guests, including the late Prime Minister's son, Sir Winston Churchill, an honorary American citizen; with President Julius K. Nyerere of Tanganyika; signing a bill into law. This page: Reviewing an honor guard with Italian Prime Minister Fanfani; presenting an award to former NATO Commander, General Lauris Norstad; with Deputy Prime Minister Sangster and Prime Minister Bustamente of Jamaica; signing the Nuclear Test Ban Treaty in 1963.

there is something the matter either with me or with the market and it's time for me to get out,' and so I did."

In 1929, when less astute businessmen were throwing themselves out of the windows of New York's skyscrapers, Joe Kennedy was counting his money and thinking about where he should go from there.

Where he went was into politics.

The intended beneficiary, of course, was Joe Kennedy. He had worked all his life to get rich and had succeeded in a big way. What he wanted now was power and fame. His work in the Roosevelt campaign was considerable enough, he reasoned, to earn him a Cabinet post. Secretary of Treasury would be nice. But one by one the Roosevelt Cabinet was

States.

He offered the benefit of his business contacts and experience and large sums of money to the Governor of New York, Franklin D. Roosevelt, who was planning to become President of The United

happened to the country. But he knew that Roosevelt was about to do something that could be the best thing that ever happened to Joe Kennedy: he was going to push for repeal of the 18th Amendment to the Constitution and make drinking legal again.

It was time to swallow some of his pride. The President's son, James, had become an insurance broker and Kennedy quietly introduced him to people who could become important clients. In the process, the insurance man became indebted to him. Once he had Jimmy Roosevelt in his hip pocket, he proposed a European vacation. For Kennedy it was a working vacation. They went to London and began calling on influential liquor distributors. Having the President's son in tow didn't hurt a bit and the important franchises he picked up included both Dewars and Haig & Haig Scotch. Later, when his son

put into place and Joe Kennedy's name wasn't even mentioned. He was entitled to some high recognition by the new Administration, but nothing they suggested was nearly high enough for Joe Kennedy.

He began grumbling publicly that Roosevelt was a terrible President and even went so far as to ask the Democrats to return some of the money he had donated to the campaign. They didn't do it, of course, and Joe decided to go back to what he had been doing before the election: making money.

He still told anyone who would listen that Roosevelt was one of the worst things that could have

Opposite page (clockwise from left): Edward Kennedy in Belgrade with Executive Council member Slavko Komar; the First Lady with French Cultural Minister Andre Malraux; the President and Princess Beatrix of Holland; Mrs. Kennedy with Mde. Andre Malraux and Mde. Harve Alphande; M. and Mde. Malraux; the Kennedys and a visitor to Washington, the Mona Lisa. This page: with the King of Laos; with the President of Venezuela; with the world champion Ratzeburg (Germany) rowing team; Robert Kennedy in Tokyo; with Laotian Prime Minister Prince Souvanna Phouma.

became President, many felt that scotch became the drink of preference in America because the Kennedy PR people had such great access to the the rest of the people – this in spite of the fact that the elder Kennedy had sold his liquor importing business for $8 million in 1946.

Once he had the franchises in hand, all he had to do was sit back and wait for Congress to get on with Repeal. But he was never one to sit back and wait. He arranged

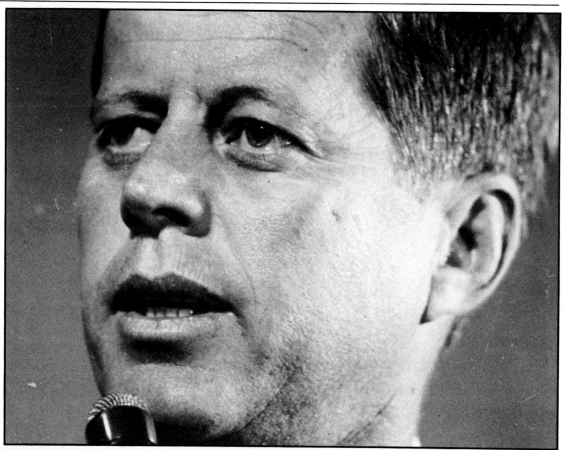

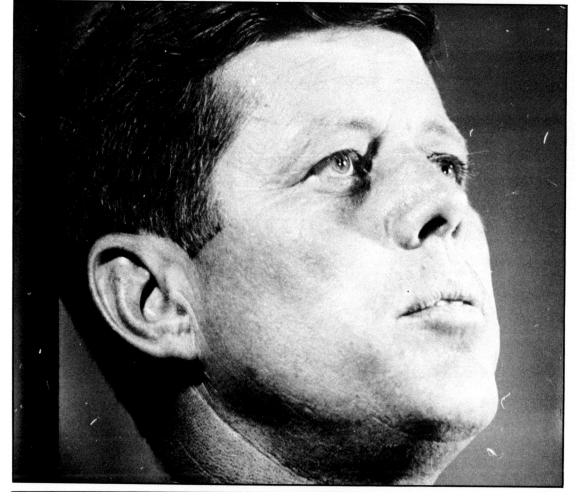

The Kennedy face was familiar in every corner of the world and the Kennedy style became known more intimately thanks to frequent trips out of Washington aboard Air Force One.

On a 1973 trip to Italy, the President was welcomed warmly by Prime Minister Leone and was the star of a reception hosted by President Segni and his wife.

to get medical permits to begin importing right away, with the result that on the day Prohibition ended, Joe Kennedy had warehouses full of scotch and gin and was, for a while at least, the only game in town.

By then he had softened his criticism of Roosevelt and the President responded with a job offer. Among the programs spawned by the New Deal was a special commission to monitor the activities of Wall Street. The new body, the Securities and Exchange Commission, would eliminate the kind of manipulation that had helped make Joe Kennedy so rich and many considered it ironic that he was named the Commission's first Chairman. During his term he inspired confidence in the business community and made a name for himself as a selfless public servant. Having done that, he said that his Government career was over for ever. And he retired one more time.

After that be became a tireless supporter of Roosevelt's New

45

On a visit to Britain, President Kennedy was welcomed by Prime Minister Harold Macmillan. In Rome, he was ushered to a private audience with Pope Paul VI by Monsignore Vivarelli. Everywhere he went, he was overwhelmed by adoring crowds.

Deal. He seemed a changed man. This same man who had unabashedly dedicated his life to making money and gathering possessions made a 1935 speech to the kids at Boston Latin School in which he told them: "...The greed of possession, the selfishness of personal acquisition, the vulgarity of mere wealth will not be the yardstick by which your efforts to succeed will be measured."

Needless to say, the President was impressed.

Through those years, Kennedy worked as a high-priced management consultant, keeping

as much time as possible free to answer any calls for help that might come from the White House. He pushed his acceptance in the Inner Circle light years ahead when he wrote a book called *I'm For Roosevelt* and paid for its publication in time for the 1936 Presidential campaign. The book was important for the President to get support from the conservative business community, which was still suspicious that the New Deal wasn't all that good for business.

The payoff after the election was the chairmanship of the Maritime Commission, a body established to

In ceremonial events, such as his arrival in West Germany, or in private moments, neither the First Lady nor the President ever seemed remotely capable of producing a dull moment.

bring some peace to an industry plagued by ruthless businessmen and militant labor unions. Once again he served with distinction, although he himself had to admit it was the toughest job he had ever been handed.

The second Roosevelt term was perceived as more anti-business than the first and Kennedy worked tirelessly to change the image.

He was clearly "owed" something. Something big. Something big came along in 1937 when the U.S. Ambassador to Britain was forced to resign for reasons of health.

For Joe Kennedy it was a plum more valuable than any Cabinet post. It represented the opportunity for the ultimate thumb-in-the-eye to the Anglophiles who ran Boston and still, after all these years, considered Joe nothing more than an Irish-Catholic upstart. He was clearly qualified and rich enough to handle the personal entertainment required. He had paid his dues, as they say, to the

Kennedy the Ambassador to Britain in 1937. War was on the horizon and the President wanted a man in Britain who wasn't likely to be too over-dazzled by British interests. His man, he announced, was Joseph P. Kennedy.

Being accepted in London was not a lot different than being accepted in Boston, but Joe

Reviewing troops, honoring police, enjoying the company of Chancellor Adenauer, the 1963 visit to West Germany seemed to suit the Kennedy style perfectly.

Administration. But there were problems, not the least of which was that Irish Catholics were no more welcome at the Court of Saint James than they were in Boston.

Many say that was the main reason why Roosevelt made

Kennedy knew many of the tricks. For his first trick, he appeared before the King to present his credentials wearing long trousers instead of the traditional knee-breeches. The court was scandalized and many said he was "not at all the type of man to represent the United States at this time." But then as now, the United States had an image with the man in the street as rambunctious, slightly vulgar and unpredictably untraditional. For them, nobody was more the type of man to represent the United States at any time than this hard-driving man from Boston who told the press he thought the Queen was "a cute trick," and from his first day in London added the term "bloody" to his incredible lexicon of tough talk.

The British people loved him, the press adored the good copy he provided them with. They were especially intrigued by his family. There were nine children to write about.

The Ambassador was doing a terrific job carrying out American policy in Britain, too. And he didn't mind telling that to any reporter who would listen. Back in Washington, the President was miffed at an Ambassador with such good press contacts, and was

careful to tell the press that Kennedy was only confirming his own views. This was after the Ambassador told a reporter that he was not "at the moment" interested in running for President himself.

As Ambassador, Kennedy was single-minded about keeping America out of the war that was breaking out in Europe. He became a strong ally of Britain's Prime Minister, Neville Chamberlain, in his attempts at appeasing Hitler. Though he gradually came to realize that war was inevitable, he regarded it as a personal mission to help Britain buy time to prepare for it. He was

When the President made a speech in front of Berlin's Brandenburg Gate, the East Germans hung drapes so he couldn't be seen on their side of the city. But in Cologne and other cities, he was welcomed by huge crowds grateful for just a glimpse.

attacked on both sides at various times. Even the President said he was "an appeaser and always will be an appeaser...and just a pain in the neck."

When war actually did break out, Roosevelt and Kennedy drifted further apart and though the Ambassador publicly supported a third term for the President, he didn't do much to scotch rumors that he himself would be a dandy candidate for the Democrats to consider. He took himself out of the race by refusing an offer to run in the Massachusetts Primary, but he

took a swipe at Roosevelt through his son Joe Jr. who, as a delegate to the Democratic National Convention, held out to the last for the nomination of James A. Farley to replace the President.

By that point, his insistence that it would be madness for America to enter the war was beginning to take the bloom off the Kennedy rose in London. The war got hot in 1940 when Hitler moved into the Scandinavian countries. Though Britain had officially been at war with Germany for eight months, this was the first time they would actually come face to face with the

enemy. Kennedy's worst fears were going to be realized, he thought. And he said so: "England lacks efficient leadership from top to bottom and unless there is a terrific change, and quickly, things will be as serious as one can imagine."

Change did come. Within a month, Chamberlain was replaced as Prime Minister by Winston Churchill, a man Kennedy had very little use for. "He's a remarkable man," admitted the Ambassador, "as remarkable as any man can be who's loaded with brandy by ten o'clock in the

The trip took him to Frankfurt, Bonn and Wiesbaden as well as Berlin and Cologne. He was accompanied by Secretary of State Dean Rusk and others.

morning." This was the same Churchill who had been instrumental in securing whiskey franchises for Kennedy a dozen years before. But Kennedy only sold the stuff, he almost never drank it. When he told the new Prime Minister that he had completely sworn off both alcohol and tobacco for the duration of the war, Churchill said, "My God, you make me feel I should go around in sackcloth and ashes."

But if Churchill and Kennedy didn't enjoy the best of friendships, Roosevelt and Churchill got along very well indeed. The result was a Kennedy

complaint circulated to newspapers back home that "as far as I can see, I'm not doing a damn thing here that amounts to anything." It was he who delivered messages from the President to the Prime Minister, but he was never told what was in them. All he knew for sure was what was contained in Churchill's responses sent back through the Embassy.

Things came to a head during the election campaign of 1940 when stories were circulated that Kennedy would be recalled to serve as Roosevelt's campaign manager while, at the same time, others were reporting that he was going to support the Republican candidate, Wendell Willkie. Neither was true, but a few days before the President was elected to his third term, his Ambassador to Britain left for home.

In France, Mrs. Kennedy's relatives in Pont Saint-Esprit followed their movements by radio. In Dunganstown, New Ross, Ireland, the President met his cousin, Mrs. Mary Ryan, In Athens, the First Lady was greeted by 12-year-old Chryssanthemi Papakotsi, whose life was saved by a heart operation arranged for her by Mrs. Kennedy.

He let the world wonder whether he'd support the President or the challenger. Up until two days before the election, very few people knew what he'd do. He had bought coast-to-coast radio time for a speech, but since he used his own money, nobody dared to even guess what he might have to say. Then, on October 29, 1940, he went on the air. But it wasn't until the end of his half-hour speech that he told his listeners, "I support the re-election of Franklin Roosevelt."

Many said it was because he was sure Willkie was more likely to involve the United States in the war. Others claimed that FDR had charmed him into thinking that he, Kennedy, could be the front-runner in 1944. The day after the election, the Ambassador formally

office building as part of the payment and suddenly discovered the heady world of real estate investing.

During the war years there was a boom in real estate in New York City and, as had so often happened before, Joe Kennedy was in on the ground floor. While he was regularly petitioning the President to give him an important Government job, he spent most of his time buying Manhattan office buildings for low prices and reselling them at huge profits. Occasionally he'd keep a promising property as a hedge against the future. In the process, he acquired huge tracts of land in Florida and Texas and then, in 1945, he bought the famous Merchandise Mart in Chicago, the

resigned and then began a tour of the country to gather support for his campaign to keep America out of Britain's war.

Once America finally did enter

the war, Kennedy volunteered to bury the hatchet and sent a message to the President that he was available to fight on any battlefront. But the plea fell on deaf ears and Kennedy was effectively sidelined. When Harry Truman became President in 1945, things didn't get any better for Joe Kennedy's effort to become a public servant again.

So he went back to doing what he knew best. Making money. During the 1960 campaign when his son was running for President, his fortune was generally valued at $400 million, though everyone who reported such figures was careful to identify them as educated guesses. What most observers do agree about, though, is that the bulk of his fortune had been earned after he came back from London and sold a house he owned in Bronxville in New York's Westchester County. He took an second largest building in the world in terms of floor space in those days. That's one of the properties the family still owns and it earns much more in a year of rent receipts than the original purchase price.

Joe Kennedy wasn't above raising rents when he bought a building, and the amount he could get away with usually determined which properties he kept and which were resold.

But if the war had presented him with opportunities for personal profit, if not for public service, it also presented him with tragedy, just as he always seems to have known it would.

In late 1940 the U.S. established a military draft. As has always been the case, the best choices

Opposite page (clockwise from left): With adoring crowds in Britain; greeting Peace Corps officials in the White House Rose Garden; Mrs. Kennedy with Queen Frederika of Greece; the President on a receiving line in West Germany. This page: In a White House ceremony; at a Paris reception; the First Lady in Istanbul; greeting Turkish officials in Washington; receiving Saint Patrick's Day shamrocks from Irish Ambassador Dr. Thomas J. Kiernan.

went to young men who volunteered rather than waiting for Uncle Sam to point a finger at them. Joe Kennedy, Jr was one who did. He was getting ready for his last year at Harvard Law School in the summer of 1941 when he decided to postpone his education and signed up in the aviation branch of the Navy.

His brother Jack had decided against law school the previous summer and had spent a semester studying business administration at Stanford University in California.

By the time Joe had made up his mind to enlist, Jack had dropped out of school and taken an extended vacation in Central and South America. When he heard that his older brother had joined up he decided to do the same thing. But rather than do exactly the same thing, he went to see an Army recruiter.

The Army rejected him because of an old football injury to his back and then so did the Navy. But he embarked on a fitness program that, in less than six months, had him back in shape and in September, two months behind his

older brother and three months before the Japanese attack on Pearl Harbor, he was accepted for duty by the Navy.

When he was a Harvard senior he had written a thesis about England's unpreparedness for war. It impressed his father's close friend, *New York Times* columnist Arthur Krock, who suggested expanding it into a book. The result was a best-seller called *Why England Slept*, published in 1940. With that behind him, the Navy decided to assign him to Washington writing special reports. He said he'd rather go to sea, but his pleas fell on deaf ears until he asked his father to use his influence.

Finally he was transferred to Newport, R.I. where he spent six months learning how to handle a PT boat. And then in 1943 he shipped out for the Pacific, a very happy young man.

In mid-summer of that same year his boat, PT-109, was rammed by a Japanese destroyer while on patrol in the Solomon Islands. There were 11 survivors, including the skipper, Lieutenant (j.g.) John F. Kennedy. After 15 hours in the water, they went ashore on an enemy-held island where they were to spend the next four days. Help finally came in response to a message Kennedy had carved on a coconut shell and slipped past the Japanese in the hands of friendly natives.

Meanwhile, the crew of PT-109 was officially listed as "missing in action," and for four days Joe Kennedy lived with the fear that his son might have been killed in the war.

His oldest son was out of harm's way at that time in Florida. But in the fall of 1943, when Jack was returned to the United States to sit out the war in a Naval hospital, Joe was sent to England where he put

On November 22, 1963, it all abruptly came to an end. Pictures of the young President were suddenly replaced by photos of the rifle that was used to kill him, by maps of where it all happened and by disbelieving faces of ordinary citizens.

REYNOLDS
RUSSELL
PATTERSON
LEWIS

JEFFERSON BLVD.

BROCK

GUINYARD
CALLAWAY

DENVER ST.

BARBARA DAVIS
VIRGINIA DAVIS

JACKET

SCOGGINS

TENTH ST.

TIPPIT

SMITH

BENAVIDES

MARKHAM

CRAWFORD ST.

PATTON AVE.

NINTH ST.

OSWALD ROUTE
Known Movements
Assumed Movements

in two six-month tours of duty, flying anti-submarine patrols over the North sea. His assignment was over and he had orders to go home when he heard about a mission that was too exciting to refuse.

By that point the Nazis were pounding London with V-2 rockets fired from a heavily fortified base on the coast of Belgium. The rockets were too fast to be tracked by radar and their home base was too tightly ringed to reach on a bombing raid. A decision was made to load a bomber with as much explosives as it could carry and crash it into the V-2 base after the two-man crew had bailed out at

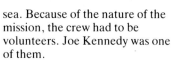

The entire world shared the grief of Edward Kennedy and other family members, and an elaborate investigation was begun at the Texas School Book Depository in Dallas to answer the question: "How?"

sea. Because of the nature of the mission, the crew had to be volunteers. Joe Kennedy was one of them.

The plane never made it across the Channel. No trace was ever found of either Joe Kennedy or his co-pilot, Lieutenant Wilford Willy. The date was August 2, 1944, one year to the day after the sinking of PT-109.

People who knew him well said that the elder Kennedy was never the same again. He spent months in seclusion and for years afterwards couldn't talk about his oldest son. Jack, now the eldest, was recovering from back injuries he had received in the Pacific and used the time to compile a book of remembrance called *As We Remember Joe*. Dozens of close friends and family members

In the next few days in Washington, as the President's body lay in the Capitol Rotunda, the central question to thousands who filed past was "Why?"

contributed to it, but Jack's own words may well have summed up the thoughts that were going through his father's mind:

"It is the realization that the future held the promise of great accomplishments for Joe that made his death so particularly hard for those who knew him. His worldly success was so assured and inevitable that his death seems to have cut through the natural order of things."

He also wrote, "I think that if the Kennedy children amount to anything now or ever amount to anything, it will be due more to Joe's behaviour than to any other factor."

The war would bring tragedy to the Kennedy family again within two short weeks.

Kathleen, the oldest daughter, had married an English peer who went on to participate in the Allied invasion of France. He was killed in action there and Kathleen left her family's side to join his family in Britain. She never went home again and in 1948 was killed in a plane crash not far from where her

While flags were lowered to half-mast all over the world, and American Embassies were crowded with mourners, Americans by the thousands descended on Washington for a final tribute to the fallen young President.

young husband had met his death.

Fifteen years later, the whole world would react in horror to the sudden death of one of Joe Kennedy's children. In fact, no American old enough to remember Friday, November 22, 1963 can forget what they were doing, where they were, at the moment they first heard that President John F. Kennedy had been shot and killed that morning in Dallas, Texas. Ironically, Joe Kennedy went to bed that night unaware of what virtually everyone in the United States already knew.

He had suffered a stroke two years before and by the end of 1963 had retired to his home in Hyannis Port, unable to speak. His wife, Rose, had received the news of her son's death from her niece who had heard it on the radio. The

As the funeral cortege moved the President's body from the White House to lie in state in the Capitol, the Kennedy children, Caroline, 6, and John, 3, accompanied it in a car with their Uncle Robert and President and Mrs. Lyndon Johnson. From that moment until the body was taken to Arlington Cemetery, the nation stood still, sharing the grief of the young family.

elder Kennedy was taking a nap and she decided not to wake him. That evening the entire household conspired to keep the news from him and it wasn't until mid-morning the following day that his youngest son, Ted, told him what had happened.

Though his doctor gave him permission to go to Washington for the funeral, he chose to stay on Cape Cod, where, like everyone across the country, he watched the sad procession on television.

As is typical of the television business, the network research departments conducted special surveys of the audience the tragedy had attracted for them. The day after the funeral, the A.C. Neilson Company reported that 93 per cent of the 4,500,000 homes in the New York metropolitan area that had TV sets were tuned in that Monday afternoon. They also reported that the average TV home had its set turned on for a total of 34 hours between Friday afternoon and Monday evening.

While all those people were absorbing so much television, hundreds of thousands had passed the catafalque, the same one that had held the body of President Lincoln 98 years before, bearing the flag-draped coffin in the Rotunda of the Capitol. The building was kept open around the clock to accomodate the silent crowds.

On Monday morning,

November 25, the body was carried from the Capitol to St. Matthew's Roman Catholic Church for a requiem mass said by an old family friend, Cardinal Richard Cushing of Boston. From there, the body was carried to Arlington National Cemetery where it was buried among the country's war dead, a stone's throw from the Lincoln Memorial.

About a million people, according to official estimates, watched the processions that day. They were joined by a host of dignitaries including the new President Lyndon Johnson, Prince Philip, husband of England's Queen Elizabeth II, President

Americans still carry indelible memories of that weekend in November, 1963. The poignancy of the young orphaned children. The solemnity of the military procession followed by a riderless horse. The sympathy for the new President and his family.

Charles De Gaulle of France, Haile Selassie of Ethiopia, Princess Beatrix of the Netherlands, President Merzagora of Italy, Ambassador Anatoly Dobrynin of the Soviet Union and former American Presidents Truman and Eisenhower.

As the body reached the gravesite 50 military jets, representing each of the states, roared overhead, followed by Air Force One, the President's

Of all the images that remain from the day of the Kennedy funeral, the one that brings more memories flooding back than almost any other, is the one of the grieving family and a final salute to his father by the three-year-old boy everyone lovingly called "John-John".

personal plane.

The New York Times commented that the funeral was "the most elaborate and impressive farewell a modern ruler has ever received."

Before being taken to the cathedral the body was taken to the White House where 220 officials of 92 nations, including eight heads of state, ten prime ministers and most of the remaining royalty in the world, had gathered to pay their respects.

When the ceremony ended, the body was taken in a solemn procession headed by military units and bands along an eight-block route to St. Matthew's. Immediately behind the caisson,

The solidarity of the Kennedy family in good times and in bad is legendary. Brothers Edward and Robert were seldom from the young widow's side during her entire ordeal.

the President's widow, Jacqueline Kennedy, was accompanied on foot by his brothers Robert and Edward. Behind them the Kennedy children, Caroline and John, followed in a limousine. The assembled dignitaries came next, led by President Johnson. *The Times* reported: "Seldom had such personages gathered at once. Certainly never had such a gathering been seen walking on foot along one of the the busiest streets in the nation."

They were followed by the Justices of the Supreme Court, in turn followed by friends of the family.

The Cathedral was filled to its

capacity of 1,100 when, at slightly after noon, the coffin was carried in, its presence having been announced by the drums and bagpipes of the Black Watch. The mass was conducted in the traditional Latin and ended with a eulogy delivered in English by the Most Rev. Philip M. Hannan, Auxiliary Bishop of Washington. It was the Bishop who sounded a

new note in the traditional display of military pageantry and religious solemnity. And he called on the dead President for his words. The eulogy was, for the most part, a quotation from Kennedy's own words of a thousand days before, when he came to Washington full of hope and dreams:

"We observe today not a victory of party but a celebration of

freedom, symbolizing an end as well as a beginning, signifying renewal as well as change.

"Let the word go forth from this time and place, to friends and foe alike, that the torch has been passed to a new generation of Americans, born in this century, tempered by war, disciplined by a hard and bitter peace, proud of their ancient heritage and unwilling to witness or permit the slow undoing of those human rights to which this nation has always been committed, and to

surround the globe. Now the trumpet summons us again – not as a call to bear arms, though arms we need, not as a call to battle, though embattled we are – but a call to bear the burden of a long twilight struggle year in and year out, 'rejoicing in hope, patient in tribulation' – a struggle against the common enemies of man: tyranny, poverty, disease and war itself.

"In the long history of the world, only a few generations have been granted the role of defending freedom in its hour of maximum

which we are committed today at home and around the world.

"Let every nation know, whether it wishes us well or ill, that we shall pay any price, bear any burden, meet any hardship, support any friend, oppose any foe to assure the survival and success of liberty.

"Let both sides unite to heed in all corners of the earth the command of Isaiah '–to undo the heavy burdens … and let the oppressed go free.'

"All this will not be finished in the first hundred days nor will it be finished in the first thousand days, not in the life of this Administration, nor even perhaps in our lifetime on this planet.

"But let us begin.

"In your hands, my fellow citizens, more than mine, will rest the final success or failure of our course.

"Since this country was founded, each generation of Americans has been summoned to give testimony to its national loyalty.

"The graves of young Americans who answered the call to service

The ceremonies were attended by the greatest gathering of world leaders in modern times as well as by thousands of Americans who lined the streets to salute the man who had changed their way of looking at life.

danger.

"I do not shrink from this responsibility – I welcome it. I do not believe that any of us would exchange places with any other people or any other generation.

"The energy, the faith, the devotion which we bring to this endeavor will light our country and all who serve it – and the glow from that fire can truly light the world.

"And so, my fellow Americans, ask not what your country can do for you, ask what you can do for

The flag that draped the casket was given to the young widow after the ceremonies according to a tradition followed for every widow of every man who has ever offered his life for his country.

your country.

"With a good conscience as our only sure reward, with history the final judge of our deeds, let us go forth to lead the land we love, asking His blessing and His help but knowing that here on earth God's work must truly be our own."

People who were in Washington on the day of the funeral remember odd little things about it. Like the fact it was a bright, sunny day, in contrast to the snowy day President Kennedy had delivered that Inaugural Address. Police on duty remember that the

Burial was in Arlington National Cemetery, the final resting place of America's honored war dead. The graveside ceremonies were conducted by Richard Cardinal Cushing of Boston, an old friend of the Kennedy family.

local crime rate dropped dramatically and that they were asked to find 121 lost children, all but one of whom were safely reunited with their families before 4:00 in the afternoon. A cab driver thought the silence was remarkable. "It's so solemn," he said, "all these thousands of people but you could hear a pin drop." Five year-old Judy Harrison of Orange, New Jersey, noticed the unusual slow marching pace of the military units and wondered why "they're dragging their feet." She told her mother she was disappointed at not having seen President Kennedy, but what she remembered most was what seems to have impressed more people about the ceremonies than anything else, the riderless horse that trotted behind the caisson carrying the coffin of the President.

It's an ancient tradition for a caparisoned, or "covered" horse to participate in the funeral of a fallen leader. In the time of such mounted warriors as Ghengis Khan, it was believed that the leader would need his horse to succeed in the after-life and his

charger was sheathed in armor and sacrificed at the warrior's funeral.

In this case, the 16 year-old chestnut stallion, whose name was Blackjack, was returned to his stable at Fort Myer, Va., at the end of the day. The saddle's stirrups were reversed, as were the boots placed in them, to symbolize that the Commander-in-Chief had fallen and would ride no more.

The Kennedy grave is marked by an eternal flame. It is one of many memorials in all parts of the world. In New Ross, Ireland, home of the Kennedy ancestors, Mary Anne Ryan, daughter of the fallen President's cousin, has a memorial in the form of an autographed picture. But, as is the case with other family members, the real memorial is in her heart.

From Berlin to Britain, and in all parts of the world, memorials in stone and bronze, place names and displays of such memorabilia as the President's famous rocking chair, have helped people remember and reflect on the life of John F. Kennedy.

The final touch in the day's ceremonies, after the 21-gun salute and the playing of taps over the gravesite, both of which are still remembered by people who were there, were six rifle volleys fired by three soldiers, commemorating the fact that the dead President was also a military veteran. Like the riderless horse, the volleys stem from an ancient tradition. When a Roman soldier was buried, it was customary for his comrades in arms to cast earth over his coffin saying the word "vale," meaning "farewell," three times.

The farewell for the fallen President extended well beyond

Washington.

In New York City thousands gathered in the main waiting room of Grand Central Terminal to share the experience on a giant TV screen. At noon, traffic was stopped and two Boy Scout buglers played taps from the marquee of the Astor Hotel in Times Square. At Idlewild Airport, soon to be renamed in honor of John F. Kennedy, all the planes on the runway were stopped as were all the trains and buses in terminals all over the city.

Schools were closed, offices shut. A downtown news-stand, deserted for the day, carried a sign that said "Closed due to a death in the American family." A boy riding his bike in the park

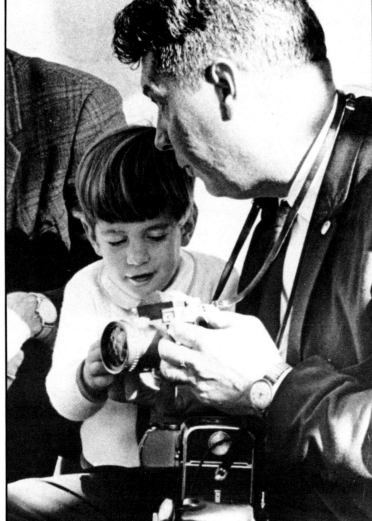

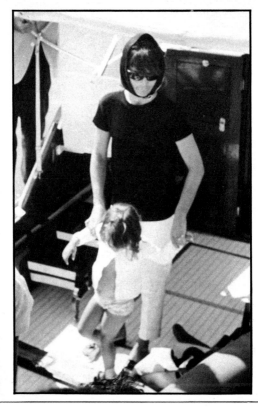

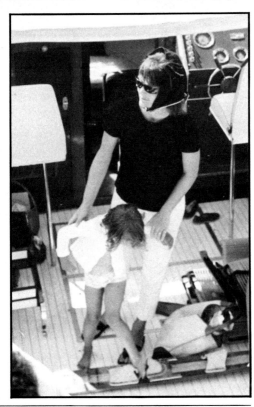

(Opposite Page): The following year, Jackie and her children John and Caroline visited her sister Princess Radziwill in Italy in the company of photographers and Secret Service agents.

explained he was there because at home "…my mother was crying, my father was crying, everybody was crying. The more I stayed around the television set, the harder it got. I had to get out and do something."

In Tokyo, thousands lined up at the American Embassy to deliver floral tributes and kept coming even after the gates had been locked. In Berlin, where he had told thousands a few months before "Ich bin ein Berliner," they

When not vacationing, the widow and children of the fallen President were at home in Georgetown in a Federal style house owned by Under Secretary of State W. Averill Harriman.

changed the name of the square in front of City Hall to John F. Kennedy Square.

Within an hour of the assassination an amateur poet expressed his feelings in verse and sent his work to *The New York Times*. Before the weekend was over, *The Times* reported having received no less than 300 such poems delivered by hand, by mail, by telegram. They came from as far away as El Salvador and from all parts of the United States, from

Clockwise from top left: Robert Kennedy in Britain with Sir Alec Douglas-Home, the Prime Minister; Robert Kennedy with Dean Sayer of the Washington National Cathedral, Chief Justice Earl Warren and others at the dedication of the Cathedral's tower; Mrs. Kennedy and Mrs. L.B. Johnson at the 1964 Democratic National Convention; Robert Kennedy campaigning in New York City.

people as young as 14 and as old as 85. Tom Lask, who was *The Times* poetry editor at the time, explained the strange phenomenon in a report that said: "Some of the writers recapitulated the killing, apparently hoping to exorcise the horrors by retelling it; others with a flicker of guilt admitted that they differed with the President, but on another level. But most seem to have written simply to express their feelings of hollowness, loss or frustration.

Clockwise from top left: President Johnson presents the Medal of Freedom in honor of the late President to Robert Kennedy; Robert Kennedy and Edward Kennedy in 1964; with Indonesia's President Sukarno; President Johnson with Robert and Ethel Kennedy.

"Many seemed to be searching for meaning in the event, pledging themselves and the nation to a more dedicated future.

"It was almost as if all these people were motivated by some archetype, some deep universal source of human utterance. Each one seemed to feel that art makes bearable what in life sometimes cannot otherwise be borne."

All of which naturally makes one wonder how anyone could want to kill this man. But the simple fact is that in the first year of his Presidency, the Secret Service investigated 870 threats to Kennedy's life. In spite of that, no one ever really tried, much to the

relief of the agents assigned to protect his life and anxious to preserve their record of not having "lost" a President since they first got the assignment in 1901 after the fatal shooting of President William McKinley.

Members of the White House detail knew they had their work cut out for them even before Kennedy took office. He had said, and meant it sincerely, that the President of The United States, as the leader of the non-Communist world, needed to appear to the world as a free man among free men and not as a man surrounded by a heavy security guard. His open car had a special removable bubble top that could deflect, if not stop, an assassin's bullet. But he made it clear that the top should be saved for a rainy day, following the lead of former President Eisenhower, who also ordered the top removed every chance he got.

In the summer of 1965, Jacqueline and children John and Caroline spent much of the time riding and relaxing at the Kennedy home in Hyannis Port, Mass.

Sometimes he even got out of his car and ran alongside. In Rome, the summer before he was killed, he gave his bodyguards instant agida when a man grabbed him around the neck, planted a big kiss on the President's cheek and then pulled him over the wooden barricade into the crowd. In Ireland, the crowd crossed the barricades and one well-wisher inadvertently knocked Kennedy off his perch into the back of the car. The week before he died, he ordered police to dispense with their usual motorcycle escort on a visit to New York. When his car was stopped for a red light, it was surrounded by young people and it

That same summer, they also took a trip to London where the children charmed the British people in much the same way as their father and his brothers and sisters had done when they were children.

took New York's Finest five minutes to get them to move so the car could move on.

In 1962 in Milwaukee a man who had had too much to drink was arrested for breaking through a

the Hearst Corporation and, because of his father's connections, was able to cover such terrific assignments as the opening of the United Nations Organization in San Francisco and

crowd and jumping onto the running board of the President's car. When they hauled him into Headquarters, he told the Sergeant at the desk, "Well, at least I got a chance to talk to the President." "Oh, Yeah," snarled the Sergeant, "and what would Mr. Kennedy have to say to you?" "He told me to go home and sober up," mumbled the defendant.

Jack Kennedy had that magnetic quality from the very start of his political life.

After he got out of the Navy in 1945 he became a journalist with

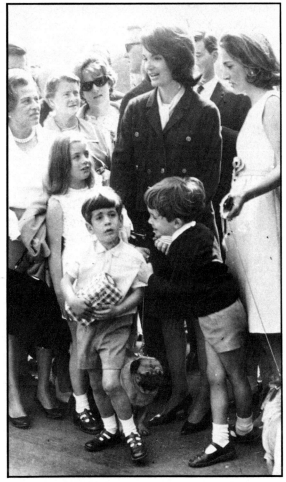

Clement Attlee's victory over Winston Churchill to become England's Prime Minister. But it wasn't his style, and more and more he began to think about politics as a career. It was built into the family tradition, after all. He took the first step in the summer of 1945 by moving back to Boston, a place where he hadn't lived, except for a few brief periods, at any time in his life.

While their Uncle Robert took care of official business, the children enjoyed the company of their aunt, Lee Radziwill, and their cousins, not to mention that of Queen Elizabeth II (who seems to have made a very interesting impression on young John).

His father moved back, too, and quietly began re-establishing contacts he knew would be necessary if his oldest son were to succeed. At the same time, both father and son watched carefully for the right opportunity.

It came in the form of no less a person than James Michael Curley, the man who had ended the political career of Patrick J. Kennedy 32 years before. In 1945, Curley decided he wanted to be Mayor of Boston again and by then the city's voters were well into the habit of giving him what he wanted.

His election to City Hall meant that he had to resign from his position as Congressman from a District that included a great many of Boston's poor Irish and Italian neighborhoods. The Kennedys decided that Jack was the ideal candidate and he announced that

The occasion on the day the Kennedys met with the Queen of England was the dedication of Britain's memorial to President Kennedy, an acre of English ground at Runnymede, near Windsor, given to the American people and set aside as a park. The night before the ceremonies, Mrs. Kennedy was entertained at dinner by Randolph Churchill, son of the late Prime Minister.

In 1966, both Robert and Edward Kennedy were members of the U.S. Senate. John and Caroline met Prince Saddrudin Khan, son of the Aga Khan, in Switzerland. And in Washington, Indira Gandhi paid tribute to the fallen President.

he would run in the Democratic Primary the following spring. Curley said anybody with the names of both Kennedy and Fitzgerald didn't even have to campaign. And everybody knew that the man who won the Primary would automatically take the election.

There was just one problem. Or rather nine. It was a ten-man race.

There was another problem, too. Jack Kennedy had probably never seen a slum in his life and, by and large, that was the battleground. But if he found it hard to visit depressing tenement buildings and shake dirty hands, he didn't let it show. And the small crowds that smiled back at him loved him for it. They gradually grew to large crowds. And so did the entourage around the candidate. He enlisted his brothers and sisters, his college friends, his Navy buddies, all of whom offered fresh faces, idealized enthusiasm and a genuine friendliness the machine politicians had abandoned years before. His father, meanwhile, paid homage to the old professionals from behind the scenes. He paid the bills, too. Some said he spent as much as $250,000 to get his son elected to Congress.

The name Kennedy itself was not exactly a drawback. Though

As Robert Kennedy met with officials in Paris and his brother Edward met in Geneva with Prince Khan, the press began circulating rumors that Jacqueline might marry Antonio Garrigues Y Canabate, Spanish Ambassador to the Holy See. Others thought her heart belonged to Prince Saddrudin Khan.

the family had moved from Boston years before, Joe Kennedy's successes in business and Government had earned him a lot of newspaper space back where he had started. Former Mayor Fitzgerald was still on the scene, still singing *Sweet Adeline*, and still reminding old-timers of the Good Old Days. And Jack's war record didn't hurt a bit.

By the time the election took place, Jack Kennedy had been to enough rallies and tea dances, had shaken enough hands and talked to enough voters to capture 40 per

cent of the vote, double the number of the next nearest contender and far ahead of the other eight hopefuls.

In the November election, almost without campaigning, he took Curley's former seat by a two-to-one margin. As would be the case when he was elected President 14 years later, he was the youngest man ever elected to the office. He was 29 years old.

In his early years as a Congressman he was alternately called a "conservative" and a "liberal", depending on who was applying the label. He seemed to vote in ways that would most please the folks back home who

As Senator from New York, Bob Kennedy dazzled his constituents with the Kennedy style and never missed an occasion to meet the people. Sometimes, as young John and Caroline found out, though it may all have been very stimulating, it could be tiring, too.

But the pace is a family tradition. Brothers Robert and Edward, Robert's wife Ethel and Jacqueline worked tirelessly unveiling memorials and meeting well-wishers, including President Jomo Kenyatta of Kenya.

would soon get another chance to vote for him. The effort paid off. He was re-elected to the Eighty-first and Eighty-second Congresses.

Then, in 1952, he raised his sights a bit higher and announced that he was going to run for the United States Senate. He had been preparing for the moment since first going to Washington. In his years as a Congressman he spent more time in Massachusetts than in the Capitol just to make sure his name and face would be well-known outside his own District.

But his Republican opponent was much better known. It was young Henry Cabot Lodge, Jr., grandson of the man who had bested Honey Fitz for the same seat back in 1916. And he himself had been serving in the Senate, except for time out to become a war hero, since 1936, having beaten the ever-present Curley.

The Republican candidate for President in the same election was also a Kennedy liability. Dwight D. Eisenhower had accepted the nomination.

During their campaign, it was tough to tell the two candidates apart in terms of their stand on issues. Both had the advantage of huge family fortunes and respected family names. But Jack Kennedy had another advantage. He was a fighter. He had shown time and again that deep inside, the race was more important to him than

graduated from law school just in time to come on board as Campaign Manager.

Candidate Lodge knew he had a tough fight on his hands, but didn't begin to worry about his chances until he realized that, as he put it, "I don't have to worry about Jack Kennedy. I don't have to worry about the Kennedy money. But I do worry about that family of his. They're all over the state!" And, he might have added, working hard enough to make a difference.

When it was all over, Eisenhower had won the Presidency by a landslide and all over the country Republicans were

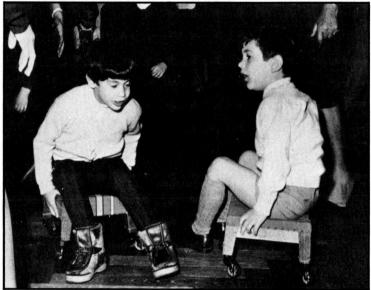

the fruits of victory. In 1952 he had the fight of his life on his hands.

His father worked hard, too, recruiting top professional help to work behind the scenes again. Outwardly, the campaign took on the same look as Jack's first run for Congress. The same fresh-faced volunteers rang doorbells and circulated petitions. But this time there was a new fresh face, Jack's younger brother Bobby had

There was time left over for vacations, too. In 1966, Mrs. Kennedy and her children spent a winter holiday in Gstaad, Switzerland, where they lived in a ten-room chalet owned by English businessman Charles Wilmers.

winning big on his coattails. But up in Massachusetts, the Republican candidate wasn't so lucky. Henry Cabot Lodge Jr. lost by more than 70,000 votes. It was an occasion for Honey Fitz to sing *Sweet Adeline* once more with feeling.

When he went to the Senate, political analysts were still busily

trying to attach a label to his philosophy. He had clearly become a liberal, but hadn't grown up that way and the establishment was slow to accept him. He was accused of being soft on the tactics of Senator Joseph McCarthy, who was making headlines by ferreting out so-called Communists. The new Senator from Massachusetts had simply avoided making any moves either for or against McCarthyism. One very good reason was that his brother Bobby was a member of McCarthy's Senate staff.

But most people, even if they didn't care much for politics, were interested in this particular politician because he was young, rich, famous, powerful, handsome and single. *The Saturday Evening Post* reported that "…Kennedy seems to be at once preoccupied,

disorganized and utterly casual – alarmingly so. For example, when he addresses the House with his shirt-tail out and clearly visible from the galleries. Many women have hopefully concluded that he needs looking after. In their opinion, he is, as a young millionaire Senator, just about the most eligible bachelor in the United States, and the least justifiable one. Kennedy lives up to that role when he drives his long convertible, hatless and with the car's top down, in Washington, or accidentally gets photographed with a glamour girl in a nightclub."

A month later, in July, 1953, *Life* magazine ran a feature article they called "Life Goes Courting

One of the Italian photographers who followed the party through the mountains reported, "she does not want to be disturbed". Which possibly explains her clenched fist.

With a U.S. Senator." The photography in this case was as far away from a nightclub as the public relations people could get. The lead to *Life's* story was: "The handsomest young member of the U.S. Senate was acting last week like any young man in love. To the family home on Cape Cod, John F. Kennedy brought his fiancée for a

Before returning home, Mrs. Kennedy and the children went on to Rome for a private audience with Pope Paul VI. At the same time, back in the United States, Robert Kennedy was following closely in his older brother's footsteps.

Two months later *Life* took its readers to the wedding of "Washington's best-looking young Senator to Washington's prettiest inquiring photographer" at the bride's mother's 300-acre Hammersmith Farm in Newport, R.I. The magazine reported that the wedding had been attended by "diplomats, Senators and social figures," and the reception for 900 good friends, including Dick and Pat Nixon, was "just like the coronation."

There were well-wishers all over the place. Thousands of curiosity-seekers had descended on Newport to peek through the fence. Many, according to one report, had chartered buses and organized special outings to share

weekend of fun. Strictly speaking the courtship of former Ambassador Joseph P. Kennedy's son and Jacqueline Bouvier terminated with the announcement of their engagement. But the courtship between the 36-year-old Massachusetts Senator and his 23-year-old fiancée goes on."

The pictures that accompanied the article showed the Senator skipping stones across the water, acting as catcher in a softball game and having his hair tousled by his bride-to-be. But she was clearly the star. She was shown sitting on the lawn and playing football with the Kennedy girls and a full-page picture of her with legs stretched out from corner to corner carried the caption: "Between games Jackie takes it easy on the veranda of the Kennedy home."

On a good will tour of Europe, Robert Kennedy visited Rome and shook hands with President Gronchi of Italy. In Athens, he signed autographs, visited the Acropolis and attended a performance by soprano Maria Callas. Sister-in-law Jacqueline had visited the same places a few months before. On another occasion (opposite page), he attended a Los Angeles benefit with former Presidential Press Secretary Pierre Salinger, Elizabeth Taylor and Mrs. John Louis.

two occasions, but miraculously survived. Unfortunately the operation wasn't a success and in mid-winter the doctors tried again. This time the surgery worked, but the recovery was worse. At one point, in fact, a priest was called to administer the Church's last rites.

Eventually the fighter in him pulled him through, even if quite slowly. Recovery took more than six months. He used the time to write another book. In it he said: "I am not sure, after nearly ten years of living and working in the midst of 'successful democratic politicians,' that they are all 'insecure and intimidated men.' I am convinced that the complication of public business and the competition for the

the moment.

Many of them were already asking each other if this man might someday be President of the United States.

But he himself wasn't so sure. He had serious health problems and the pain was getting worse. The football injury that had nearly kept him out of the service, combined with injuries he suffered in the war, had made him a virtual cripple by the time he celebrated his first wedding anniversary. Doctors advised surgery, but grimly told him that he had almost no chance of surviving an operation. It was a tough decision to make, but in the fall of 1954 he went to New York to have it done. During his recovery from the double fusion of spinal discs he appeared to be dying on at least

public's attention have obscured innumerable acts of political courage – large and small - performed almost daily in the Senate Chamber. I am convinced that the decline – if there has been a decline – (in the public's judgment of professional politicians) has been less in the Senate than in the public's appreciation of the art of politics, of the nature and necessity for compromise and balance, and the nature of the Senate as a legislative chamber. And I am convinced that we have criticized those who have followed the crowd – and at the

In 1967, Jacqueline and the children visited the Kennedy ancestral home in County Wexford, Ireland, an occasion for the young widow to meet her late husband's living relatives. Caroline, at the same time, was beginning to get into the swing of ceremonial functions such as launching ships.

same time criticized those who have defied it – because we have not fully understood the responsibility of a Senator to his constituents or recognized the difficulty facing a politician conscientiously desiring, in Daniel Webster's words, 'to push his skiff from the shore alone' into a hostile and turbulent sea. Perhaps if the American people more fully comprehended the terrible pressures which discourage acts of political courage, which drive a Senator to abandon or subdue his conscience, then they might be less critical of those who take the easier road – and more appreciative of those still able to follow the path of

Jacqueline, meanwhile, kept up her pace of public appearances, but with Caroline to help, she had more time for private pleasures such as horseback riding.

The hottest rumor of early-1968 was that Jackie would soon marry Britain's Lord Harlech. Though photographers and reporters followed them through a visit to Cambodia, neither she nor he would confirm or deny it.

courage."

The book, a collection of examples of politicians responding to crises, was called *Profiles in Courage*. It was a popular success, especially after it earned the Pulitzer Prize in 1957.

With it the Senator had pushed his skiff from the shore and was beginning to look more Presidential ever day.

The opening salvos were fired in Chicago at the 1956 Democratic National Convention. President Eisenhower was the obvious choice of the Republicans to run for a second term and the Democrats were putting their

to get to look more Presidential. He made good use of the time.

In 1958, *The New York Times* reported that "invitations to make speeches, accept honorary degrees, appear on television or to grace a staggering number of dedications, mortgage burnings, clambakes and other public festivities pour into his office at the rate of about 500 each month."

Many said he was pushing too hard to be in the limelight. It was a foregone conclusion that Vice President Nixon would be the Republican choice in 1960, but Mr. Nixon was taking a far different approach. It was conceded that the

hopes on Adlai Stevenson who had been buried in the 1952 Eisenhower landslide.

Stevenson had let it be known that rather than hand-picking his running mate, as is customary, he would let the Convention delegates decide for themselves who would be their candidate for Vice President.

Jack Kennedy smelled an opportunity. Armed with his

courage and his brother Bobby, he went to Chicago to do some arm-twisting. It was heady stuff and they seemed to enjoy every minute of it. But this wasn't Boston and a more seasoned veteran of national politics, Senator Estes Kefauver of Tennessee, took the prize from their hands. But they gave him a good run for his money and in the process gained for themselves valuable national attention.

The Stevenson-Kefauver ticket wasn't good enough to beat Eisenhower and his Vice President Richard Nixon, and it was fairly certain that if Kennedy had been the Convention's choice, it wouldn't have made a bit of difference – except to make Jack Kennedy look like a loser when the Democrats met again in Los Angeles in 1960.

And it gave Kennedy four years

Vice President was even more sought-after for public appearances than the Senator, but he chose to reject most of the invitations. Nixon had the image of a free-swinging politician and was quietly working to take on the appearance of a mature statesman. He wasn't sure he'd have to face the Senator from Massachusetts two years hence, but he was clearly setting himself up to be a contrast

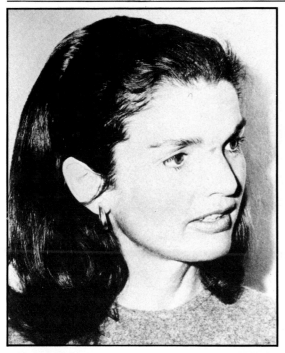

In 1968, all the marriage rumors were put to rest when Jackie and her children went to the Greek Island of Skorpios and she married Aristotle Onassis. That same year, she and Robert Kennedy went to Atlanta for the funeral of Dr. Martin Luther King, also the victim of an assassination, and in March, 1968, Robert Kennedy announced that he was challenging President Johnson for the leadership of the Democratic Party.

to the boyish Jack Kennedy.

In the Senate, Kennedy began exerting his leadership and making moves to identify himself with the liberals and the internationalists in his party. He took strong stands on foreign affairs, welfare and labor reform. He took a trip around the world with his wife and when he came back warned the country (to their surprise) that the French were about to lose out in Indochina. He began building a highly-professional staff, just as his father had done on the campaign front, including young professors from several Ivy League universities.

If all the effort was undertaken with an eye on the Presidency, it didn't hurt a bit when the Senator ran for re-election in Massachusetts in 1958. He won by almost 875,000 votes, the biggest margin of victory in the history of the State.

Only one thing stood in his way by that point: his religion. It was a fact that no Catholic had ever been elected President. And that fact was no accident of fate.

Hardly a story was written about him in newspapers or magazines that didn't raise the issue. Most were in the vein of a profile in *The Economist* which said, "There is irony in this issue because Mr. Kennedy, like most of his rivals in both parties, is close to being a

On June 7, 1968, tragedy struck the Kennedy family and the nation again. Senator Robert Kennedy was shot and killed by an assassin in Los Angeles, California. His grave, near his brother's in Arlington National Cemetery, is still the site of frequent memorial services.

spiritually rootless modern man. He performs the prescribed devotions of his faith, but his accession to the Presidency would no more mean 'the Pope in the White House' than the election of an Episcopalian would signify the coming to power of the Archbishop of Canterbury."

But the issue remained. And it made the party's hierarchy a bit nervous. It was clear that Kennedy had to prove it wouldn't make any difference and it would take more than just speeches and well-placed news stories to do that.

He had to take the issue to the voters. He formally announced that he was indeed a candidate on the day after New Year's in 1960. In February he ran against Minnesota Senator Hubert Humphrey in the Primary in Wisconsin. He felt that a good showing in a heavily Protestant Midwestern state would effectively

put religion out of the campaign. The two men slugged it out for a month, reaching every corner of the state in spite of bitter cold and heavy snow. When the votes were counted Kennedy had won. But Humphrey said he wasn't out of the race yet because the margin was very close. And the political professionals still weren't convinced that Kennedy's lead wouldn't have been bigger if he hadn't been a Catholic.

They decided the issue would be better settled in West Virginia. The pros perceived it to be a hotbed of anti-Catholic sentiment and Humphrey's supporters were sure that their man would have strong appeal in a state with such a high unemployment rate. Humphrey ran hard against the

Leadership of the family fell on the shoulders of Senator Edward Kennedy aided by his wife, Joan. Young John F. Kennedy Jr., meanwhile, was growing up fast.

Along with the responsibility, Ted Kennedy also inherited the Kennedy popularity and attracted admiring crowds wherever he went.

Kennedy wealth. Kennedy ran hard against religious bias.

The Kennedy machine rolled all over the state. Although money was an issue, it was clearly no object. And the professional organization the Kennedys had put together was too overwhelming for the Senator from Minnesota. Humphrey lost big. It marked the end of his Presidential aspirations. But before he retired from battle, this man, who had started out as the owner of a small drugstore, sounded a warning for any other candidate with the temerity to take on Jack Kennedy when he said, "I feel like the owner of a mom and pop store who has to compete with a chain store."

The Kennedy bandwagon rolled through five other states before

century. Kennedy had shown them how to use television, how to make polling an effective tool, how to orchestrate a campaign to the very best advantage. Money has power, the Kennedy men agreed, but knowing how to spend it was what the game was all about.

He would give them a first-hand demonstration in the fall of 1960. The turning point of the campaign was a device Kennedy had used effectively in Massachusetts in the campaign against Henry Cabot Lodge: a televised debate. Though candidate Nixon had spent several years trying to change his image, he couldn't hide his pedantic side and couldn't help moralizing a bit too much. He also had the problem of not looking all that terrific on television. All things considered, the four face-to-face debates between Kennedy and Nixon that were seen by millions probably made the difference.

Convention time and he won in every one of them. They went to Los Angeles with all but about 150 of the total number of votes they'd need to sew up the nomination. The old professionals were still skeptical and couldn't help grumbling that this was less a display of vote-getting power than of the power of money. But what they didn't realize was that politics had finally entered the 20th

(Opposite page, from top left): Mrs. Rose Kennedy at the 1971 opening of the John F. Kennedy Center For The Performing Arts in Washington; Mrs. Kennedy and Maestro Leonard Bernstein; Edward Kennedy; the Edward Kennedy family arriving with his mother at the Kennedy Center. (This page, from top left): Joseph Kennedy, son of Robert Kennedy, in 1972; Senator Ted Kennedy; the Senator visiting Israel; Joseph Kennedy after being freed from a hijacked airliner; at a Christmas party for New York ghetto children; Joan Kennedy.

And the difference was important. More people voted for a new President in 1960 than in any election up to that time. But the vote was closer than in almost any other election, too. Jack Kennedy went to bed the night the votes were counted not knowing whether he had won or lost. And it wasn't until late the next morning that Nixon finally conceded. Kennedy's margin of victory was slightly more than 118,000 votes, two-tenths of a percent of the total. Mr. Nixon's running mate, incidentally, was none other than Henry Cabot Lodge, the former Senator from Massachusetts.

Kennedy's main support came from the big industrial states in the Northeast, just where the pros always knew it would, but he got a big boost in the South, too. Thanks

for that went to his running mate, Lyndon Johnson, hand-picked by Kennedy "for the good of the party," despite the fact that the Senate Majority Leader had wanted the top spot for himself and had said some unkind things about the Kennedy family in the process, a totally unforgivable offense to any Kennedy.

A short time after he was elected, Kennedy told a reporter, "Sure it's a big job. But I don't know anybody who can do it any better than I can. I'm going to be

Clockwise from top left: Senator Kennedy with Presidential candidate George McGovern; Teddy Kennedy, Jr; Ted Kennedy with the wife of the German Foreign Secretary; Ted Kennedy campaigning; David Kennedy, son of Robert Kennedy.

in it for four years. It isn't going to be so bad. You've got time to think – and, besides, the pay is pretty good."

A year later he wasn't quite as optimistic. "The job is interesting," he said, "but the possibilities for trouble are unlimited. It represents a chance to exercise your judgement on matters of importance. It takes a lot of thought and effort. It's been a tough first year. But then, they're all going to be tough."

Things got really tough three

of Pigs.

The invasion was a complete disaster and within three days Fidel Castro had taken most of the invaders prisoner. An aide close to the President said "this is the first time Jack Kennedy ever lost anything."

And he didn't like the idea of losing at all. He needed a new world to conquer and decided to take advantage of an opportunity to meet Soviet Premier Nikita Khrushchev in Vienna. It turned out not to be a golden opportunity at all.

months into the new Administration. On April 17, 1961 about 1400 Cuban exiles, armed with American weapons and trained by the Central Intelligence Agency, invaded Cuba. The plot had been hatched during the

Eisenhower Administration, but the new President didn't do anything to stop it beyond eliminating planned protective air cover and switching the invasion site from a small city to a deserted beach at a place known as the Bay

By the early 1970's, all the Kennedy children were beginning to resent being called children. From top left: Caroline; Caroline with her cousin, Robert Kennedy,

Jr.; John; and Robert Kennedy, Jr. with a falcon and with a puff adder while filming a television series in Kenya.

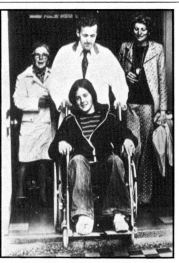

The President had been planning a European trip for some time. He had scheduled a meeting with Charles de Gaulle in Paris and another with Harold Macmillan in London. Except for a visit to Canada, it would be his first trip out of the country.

In spite of the Cuban fiasco, the Gallup organization, which regularly measures a President's popularity, had given him the news that a whopping 83 percent of the voters thought he was doing a good job. He knew that the impromptu meeting with the Russian leader would have a serious impact on how the rest of the world would perceive the job he was doing. In

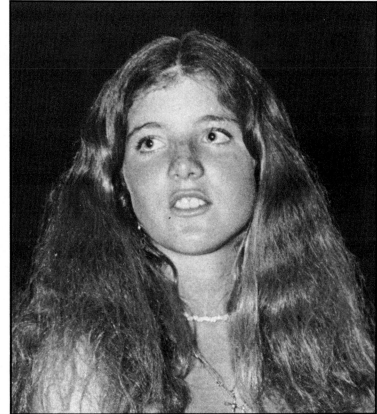

From top left: Ted Kennedy and sister Patricia Lawford await word on his son Edward whose leg was amputated because of cancer; Ted's daughter, Kara in a wheelchair after an accident with a horse-drawn carriage; Ethel Kennedy; Jacqueline Kennedy Onassis; Caroline Kennedy; Caroline at the 1974 Robert Kennedy Memorial Tennis Match; and with Mrs. Pierre Trudeau. Opposite: The family gathers at President Kennedy's grave on the anniversary of his death.

anticipation, he spent weeks studying the Khrushchev personality. And in the history of the world, there were probably never two such important leaders with such diverse personalities.

Nikita Khrushchev was 67 years old at the time, compared to Kennedy's 44. The Soviet Premier was the son of a miner, had not been able to read or write until after he was 20 years old, and had scratched his way to the top of the Byzantine labyrinth of the Communist Party organization in Moscow. He had held the job for

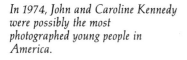

In 1974, John and Caroline Kennedy were possibly the most photographed young people in America.

John, a budding tennis player, was almost 14 then. His sister Caroline was 16 going on 17.

six years by then.

The American President was the son of a millionaire, had been educated in the best schools. Though he had legislative experience and had shown himself to be both cool and hard-headed, he was quite new at the game of international politics. On taking office, for instance, he had requested that the Communists should honor a six-month moratorium on their international activities, a request that added funny grins to the faces of the men who were directing the takeover in Laos.

Kennedy wanted the Vienna meeting so he could see for himself what he was up against. For his part the wily old Russian seemed to want to find out for himself if the new American President was really as naive as he appeared. They both learned a lot. For Kennedy's part, he found that Khrushchev was a good deal tougher than any of his research had told him. The talks led nowhere except for an agreement to a cease-fire in Laos, which was never honored. They ended with Khrushchev's refusal to back down

on a plan to sign a peace treaty with East Germany, which could have a serious impact on the status of Berlin.

At one point during the talks, Kennedy noticed that among the military decorations the Premier

Senator Ted Kennedy and his wife, Joan, in 1976.

wore on his chest was the Lenin Peace Prize. "I hope you get to keep it," he said grimly.

The trip wasn't a total failure, though. His three days in Paris had been a triumph. The First Lady, who had attended the Sorbonne and spoke fluent French, stole the show at a glittering round of parties and receptions. It prompted her husband to preface a Paris speech, "I do not think it is altogether inappropriate to

In 1973, Kathleen Kennedy, daughter of Robert Kennedy, was married. Her Uncle Ted gave the bride away. Her cousin, Teddy Jr. acted as unofficial photographer. Her aunt Joan provided an extra touch of glamor.

The entire family, including Jackie's mother, Mrs. Hugh Auchincloss, gathered to celebrate the day in 1975 when Caroline graduated from Concord Academy in Massachusetts.

introduce myself to this audience. I am the man who accompanied Jacqueline Kennedy to Paris, and I have enjoyed it."

After he got back, the Russians kept insisting on the East German treaty and he, just as doggedly, kept insisting that Berlin must be kept free. "We don't want to fight," he said, "but we have fought before. We cannot and will not permit the Communists to drive us out of Berlin."

If he learned nothing more from his Vienna experience, John F. Kennedy learned the valuable lesson that the Communists had the idea that words meant very little and that American threats would never be backed up with real force. He knew that if push came to shove, he would have to shove back.

When the Communists began shoving by blockading Berlin, Kennedy's shove back came in the form of an order to send an American armored convoy through East German territory into the threatened city. Though

Clockwise from top left: John and Caroline; Ethel and Ted; Mrs. Jacob Javits and Joan; Pat Lawford and Ethel; Pat Lawford, Caroline and Ted; Joan.

the journey turned out to be an anticlimax, it involved a strong risk of provoking fighting, and the message to the Communists didn't go unnoticed.

A similar, much more dramatic confrontation would take place much closer to home in late summer, 1962. In August, a U.S. plane was fired on off the Cuban coast. In October, the President went on national television to announce that the Soviet Union had established missile bases in Cuba and that an official American

The event was the 1974 Robert F. Kennedy Tennis Tournament at Forest Hill, N.Y. According to an old family tradition, the Kennedys were as much participants as spectators.

blockade would go into effect immediately. It was one of the most dramatic speeches of Kennedy's career. Two days later, *The New York Times* said: "When President Kennedy made his address to the nation, retail stores, Broadway theaters, motion picture houses and other places of entertainment reported declines in patronage. Yesterday people seemed to be going about their affairs. Department stores reported that there had been no 'panic' buying of articles that might be in limited supply in wartime."

Ted Kennedy with his wife Joan and with his son Teddy, Jr.; Rose Kennedy with son-in-law Sargent Shriver. At the President's grave with French President Giscard d'Estaing.

There was clearly a feeling of disaster in the air. Fidel Castro shouted that any Americans headed for Cuba had better come ready for war. An American Defense Department official confirmed that ships involved in the blockade were empowered to sink any ship headed for Cuba that refused to be boarded. When U.N. Ambassador Adlai Stevenson introduced photographic proof of the missile buildup 90 miles from the American mainland, the Secretary General called for, and got, a Soviet promise to suspend

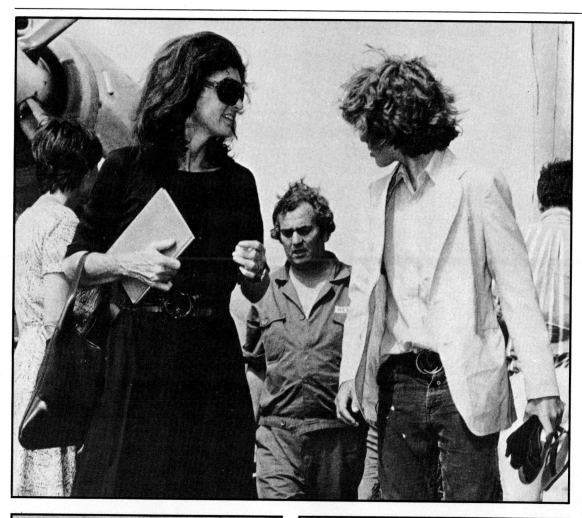

arms shipments. But that wasn't good enough for President Kennedy. He wanted the missiles already there withdrawn right away. Khrushchev's response was an offer to withdraw if the U.S. would take its missiles out of Turkey. Once again the President

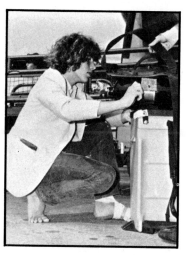

Jacqueline arriving with John and Caroline at the Onassis-owned private island of Skorpios in 1975 for a much-needed rest.

refused to accept the Russian terms, but suggested that if the Russians removed the missiles, he'd remove the blockade and agree never to invade Cuba. Khrushchev grudgingly agreed and two weeks after the crisis began, it ended with a stunning victory for the President.

Within a few more weeks the Cold War took on a whole new aspect. The Communists in Peking began making noises that the

Kremlin was getting soft on Capitalism. The Russians began talking about peace as though they really meant it, even asking for new ideas to stop nuclear testing. And in Berlin, a new crisis vanished without a trace.

And best of all, in an unusual outpouring of support, the voters elected most of the President's preferred candidates (including his younger brother, Ted, newly

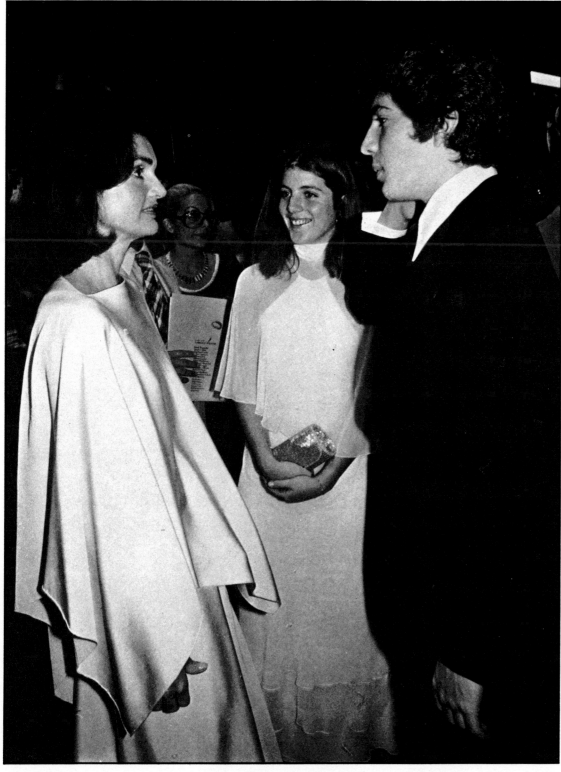

Opposite page, clockwise from top left: With Chinese Foreign Minister Huang Hua; with Egyptian President Anwar El Sadat; at work in the Senate; with sister Jean and her husband Stephen Smith; Michael, son of Robert Kennedy; Joan and Ted at the President's grave. This page: Jacqueline with Caroline and John; John at 17; Ethel and son Joe.

elected to the Senate in Massachusetts) in the Congressional elections a couple of weeks later, breaking a tradition of going against the President in off-year elections. Among the losers was Kennedy's old friend, Richard M. Nixon, who, after conceding defeat, told reporters that they "won't have Nixon to kick around any more."

There was very little doubt in anyone's mind, at that point, that Kennedy would run for a second term. The only real question the political pundits felt compelled to wrestle with was who the Republicans might nominate to run against him. The smart money was on New York's Governor, Nelson Rockefeller, who had just rolled up an impressive half-million-vote margin to win the fall election. That scenario was never to be played out, of course, but the prospect of two millionaire candidates going head to head in a national election was very heady stuff, indeed.

Halfway through his Administration, Jack Kennedy was more popular than ever. He had matured more than anyone could have imagined possible and he had earned the respect, if not the complete support, of the leaders of

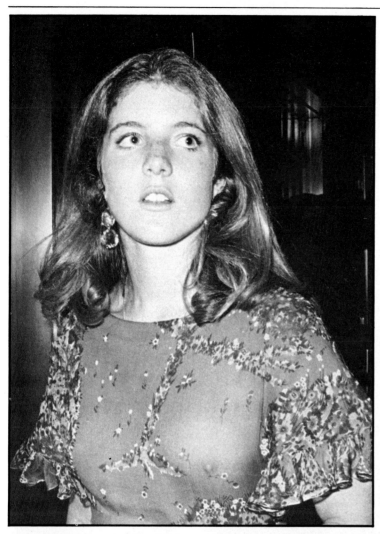

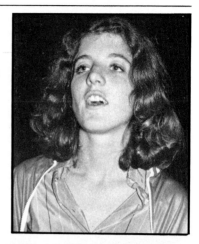

running strong."

His record on domestic issues wasn't quite as wonderful. He had inherited a mild recession from the Eisenhower Administration, but in the two years it had ended. Critics contended that he had nothing to do with that, though, and then went on to count off some of the other problems the President would have to solve if he wanted another four years in the White House. Unemployment, for instance, was high. The balance of payments problem didn't seem to be going away fast enough. There

the free world. He had built up the country's defenses and taken a lot of the bite out of the Russian bear. Nobody would think of challenging him when he said in the State of the Union message that "our tide is

In the late 1970's, Caroline and John became a familiar part of the New York disco scene. Occasionally, Robert Kennedy, Jr., joined them in the company of model Cheryl Tiegs. Robert also frequently escorted black model Jules Dreyfus. His cousins Caroline and John kept the marriage predictors guessing, too. As did Ted Kennedy, Jr., who sometimes appeared with his mother, Joan; and 24-year-old David, son of Robert Kennedy, never seemed to be without a pretty girl, either.

was a need to do something more to improve the quality of education, and the big cities seemed on the verge of going down the drain.

It all sounds familiar twenty years later, as does the cry of a 1963 editorial writer to do something about "the alarming wastage of young people in delinquency, unemployment and apathy."

But at the beginning of '63, the President was confident he could do something about most of these problems. The international tensions that had preoccupied him had cooled and for the first time he would be working with a Congress he considered friendly.

At the same time, there seemed to be a youth movement in the House and Senate. A combination of death, defeat and retirement had eliminated a host of older, more conservative people in Congress, opening spots on

important committees to people more likely to be cooperative with this vigorous and inventive Chief Executive. The recent election had not only given him more such people, but confirmed his popularity in the only way professional politicians understand: with votes. In his first two years, the narrow margin of his own victory was justification for many in Congress to be less than cooperative because of the lack of a clear mandate.

As Tom Wicker pointed out in

In 1980, Ted Kennedy announced that he would run in Presidential Primaries against President Jimmy Carter, an attempt that ended in failure.

The Times in 1963, "There is little doubt that the John F. Kennedy of today is a more confident man, a surer-handed executive, a more forceful leader than the young Senator who bounced into office in 1961. He is, in fact, at last the President of the United States."

But if Washington changed Jack Kennedy, the changes he brought to the city itself were enormous and it is thanks to him that the Washingtonians of today have a cultural life they can be proud of.

When the Kennedy presidency began, with the participation at the Inaugural of the poet Robert Frost, the District of Columbia was regarded all over the world as a cultural wasteland. The Times of

But the Primary campaign that year, as is the case with every other Kennedy campaign, was a total family affair.

London said that "Washington society prefers talk to listening, and the performing arts suffer."

In 1961, the city had one experimental theater: the Arena Stage, one commercial playhouse: the National, one Opera company: the Opera Society, and a symphony orchestra: the National Symphony, which was not regarded by any orchestra in the country to be serious competition. The Capitol had a ballet company that scheduled performances a couple of times a year. In terms of culture, the only serious efforts in the city were its art galleries and chamber music groups.

The Federal Government, moreover, reflected the effects of all this and did very little to support any of the arts. Once when it was suggested in Congress that financial aid for the arts might be the right thing to do, one of the statesmen there suggested that he regarded poker playing to be a serious art form, and wouldn't support any such legislation unless

This page, from top: Caroline and Ted; Caroline at age 23; Caroline with boyfriend, Tom Carney; Joan in Athens with hostess Kara-Anne Latasis. Opposite page: Caroline and Tom Carney; Caroline at the wedding of her cousin Michael; John Kennedy, Jr.; Ted celebrating his 50th birthday with son Edward and daughter Kara; Ted and Joan at Michael's wedding.

it included funds to keep the game going.

It was always traditional for Presidents to plan entertainments for state dinners, but since the days of Thomas Jefferson, who many said was the last cultured President, most had interpreted that to mean popular entertainments. In the Eisenhower years, foreign dignitaries were subjected to American television stars.

But Kennedy changed all that by

The redecoration included the installation of a stage for the first time in the history of the building and Presidential invitations to use it ranged from Shakespearean production to jazz concerts.

The President and the First Lady took the cause out of the White House, too, and began attending performances of the National Symphony (an orchestra which has become, 20 years later, a major force in the world of music) and of the Opera Society. And he took a strong public stand in favor of the

inviting such people as Pablo Casals and Ralph Richardson, Carl Sandberg and Igor Stravinsky to his command performances. For the first time since Jefferson, America's Capital could compete with Paris and London in its encouragement of the arts. And all the arts were considered. Jacqueline Kennedy took on the job of turning the White House into the showplace it was intended to be by furnishing it with authentic American antiques. She also decorated the walls of the family rooms with French Impressionist art, as well as some paintings she did herself. creation of a multi-million dollar National Cultural Center that would become a home for all these institutions, and more, in the heart of Washington. It would later become the John F. Kennedy

Center for the Performing Arts.

The ideas didn't go down easily in some circles. Many Americans seriously considered symphonic music a bore, ballet effete, and experimental theater not worth the trouble. His critics called him an

"egghead" and said such efforts would never play in Peoria. In the hands of another President, they may have been right. But President Kennedy had other interests, too. He loved red-blooded movies like "Spartacus" and let it be known that among the thousands of words he read every day, the James Bond novels were often the most fun. Both he and his wife were also responsible for creating another new interest in America: physical culture. Harry Truman had been a proponent of taking long walks and Ike spent long hours on the golf course, but few Presidents before Kennedy had done as much toward making Americans want to get out and exercise and get themsleves into good physical shape as Jack Kennedy. The image that side of him projected, in addition to making us a nation of joggers,

Twenty years after the assassination of the President: Ted, Jackie, Caroline and John, Jr.

made the folks out in Peoria sit up and take notice. Suddenly culture wasn't something you participated in once in a while to keep your wife happy or to impress the neighbors that you weren't some kind of a boor. After all, he said, "it is tremendously important that we regard music not just as part of our arsenal in the cold war, but as an integral part of a free society."

There are all kinds of facets to the Kennedy legacy. He left us

richer for having known him. In his days as President, he made us proud to be Americans, happy to be alive. Before he came on the scene, people used to wear little buttons with a smile on them. When Kennedy was President, they went out of style in favor of smiles on people's faces.

In *Profiles in Courage*, Kennedy had deplored the fact that polls showed that while contemporary parents still hoped that their

favorite children would fulfill the American dream by someday becoming President, an alarming number of them said that the last thing they wanted to become was a politician. When he became President himself, the profession of politics became much more honored than it had been for a long, long time.

In the years since, we've had five different Presidents, each with his own personal style, each with his own set of problems, each leaving a stamp on the American way of looking at life. But few Presidents, before or after Kennedy, gave us a model to follow that made life quite as enjoyable, that made us feel that this really was the greatest country in the history of the world and that there could be joy in making it even better.

A few weeks after his assassination, Jacqueline Kennedy was interviewed for *Life* magazine by the historian Theodore H. White. What she told him has become for most people who remember President Kennedy fondly the perfect description of how we all felt:

"All I keep thinking of is this line from a musical comedy," she said. "At night before we went to sleep, Jack liked to play some records, and the song he loved most came at the very end of this record. The lines he loved to hear were, 'Don't let it be forgot, that once there was a spot, for one brief shining moment that was known as Camelot.'"